GAME ON

Using Digital Games to Transform Teaching, Learning, and Assessment

RYAN L. **SCHAAF**
NICKY **MOHAN**

Solution Tree | Press

a division of
Solution Tree

555 North Morton Street
Bloomington, IN 47404
800.733.6786 (toll free) / 812.336.7700
FAX: 812.336.7790

email: info@SolutionTree.com
SolutionTree.com

Visit **go.SolutionTree.com/technology** to download the free reproducibles in this book.

Printed in the United States of America

20   19   18   17   16   1   2   3   4   5

Library of Congress Control Number: 2016951886

Solution Tree

Jeffrey C. Jones, CEO
Edmund M. Ackerman, President

Solution Tree Press

President: Douglas M. Rife
Editorial Director: Tonya Maddox Cupp
Managing Production Editor: Caroline Weiss
Senior Production Editor: Suzanne Kraszewski
Copy Chief: Sarah Payne-Mills
Proofreader: Evie Madsen
Text and Cover Designer: Abigail Bowen
Editorial Assistants: Jessi Finn and Kendra Slayton

I dedicate this book to Connor, Ben, and the rest of the digital generation. Special thanks to my wonderful wife, Rachel. To a sensational mentor, Linda Tsantis—many thanks for your support and friendship. You are my world! Ian and Nicky—your friendship is always appreciated and never taken for granted.

—Ryan L. Schaaf

To my late husband, Mini, whose support and love I will always treasure. Thank you for your constant encouragement. You continue to be my inspiration and motivation to move my career forward. You are my rock. I dedicate this book to you.

To my daughter, Shona—you are my everything under the sun. You continue to grow into one of the most beautiful, intelligent, amazing, and strong women I have ever known. To my son, Sherwen—you are an incredible young man. Your strength, wit, intellect, creativity, and sense of humor never cease to amaze me. To Shane—you are loving and caring and have a heart of gold. To Mahla—I couldn't be prouder of you. Thank you for making me smile and for encouraging me.

To my Mum, Chand, Dad, and Suraj, for their steadfast love and support. To my sister, Reena; my brother-in-law, Nishan; my nephew, Renae, and his wife, Lesley; my niece, Bhavna; and my sister-in-law, Fatima; for always being there, supporting me in all of my endeavors, convincing me to believe in myself, and always believing in me even when I did not. To baby Kriday, for bringing so much joy into our lives.

To Barbara Woods, my cherished friend. An educator of superb skill and perfect integrity, a trusted confidante, and a real mensch, whose encouragement, emotional support, good advice, and good cheer have helped me all through the years.

To Ian, whose help and encouragement to explore new horizons made the idea of writing this book possible. You have the biggest heart, always giving of yourself and making the time to make me feel special. You are one in a million!

—Nicky Mohan

ACKNOWLEDGMENTS

We thank Ian Jukes for his continued support and guidance and Ted McCain for his wonderful insights into modern learning. A special thanks to Lori Gerstein Ramsey, Victoria Van Voorhis, Anne Snyder, and Trish Cloud for their insights and reactions to *Game On*.

Solution Tree Press would like to thank the following reviewers:

Russell Brandon
Educational Technology Coordinator
St. Francis Xavier School
Phoenix, Arizona

Iram Khan
Principal
McLeod Road Traditional School
Surrey, British Columbia, Canada

Trish Cloud
Technology Associate and Technology
  Contact
Grand Oak Elementary
Huntersville, North Carolina

Jonathan Spike
Technology Integrator
Green Bay Area Public Schools
Green Bay, Wisconsin

Linda T. Darcy
Director of Human Capital
  Development
Newington Public Schools
Newington, Connecticut

Visit **go.SolutionTree.com/technology** to download
the free reproducibles in this book.

TABLE OF CONTENTS

ABOUT THE AUTHORS

 **Ryan L. Schaaf** is an instructional designer and graduate faculty member for the Johns Hopkins School of Education. Previously, he was assistant professor of educational technology at Notre Dame of Maryland University. He has more than eighteen years of experience in the field of education. Before higher education, Ryan was a public school teacher, instructional leader, curriculum designer, and technology integration specialist in Maryland. In 2007, he was nominated as Maryland Teacher of the Year.

Ryan enjoys presenting sessions and workshops about the potential for gaming in the classroom, the characteristics of 21st century learning, and emerging technologies and trends in education. Ryan has published several research articles related to the use of digital games as an effective instructional strategy in the classroom in *New Horizons for Learning* and the *Canadian Journal of Action Research*. His first book, *Making School a Game Worth Playing: Digital Games in the Classroom*, which he coauthored with Nicky Mohan, was published in 2014. He also authored *Using Digital Games as Assessment and Instruction Tools*. He coauthored his third book, *Reinventing Learning for the Always-On Generation: Strategies and Apps That Work*, with Ian Jukes and Nicky Mohan.

To learn more about Ryan's work, follow @RyanLSchaaf on Twitter.

 **Nicky Mohan** is the cofounder and managing partner of InfoSavvy21, an international educational consulting firm. At InfoSavvy21, her focus is on developing real-world just-in-time teaching and learning experiences that are relevant to both teachers and students. She has been a classroom teacher, school and university administrator, instructional designer, business sector manager and trainer, and an international speaker. At the University of Waikato, New Zealand, she designed and delivered courses and workshops based on research of best practices in teaching and learning.

Since 2006, she has made hundreds of presentations in more than a dozen countries. Sharing her time between Canada and New Zealand, Nicky worked as the director of curriculum for the 21st Century Fluency Group, leading a team of international writers as the creative force behind the designing of lesson plans. Nicky is the coauthor of *Making School a Game Worth Playing: Digital Games in the Classroom* and *Reinventing Learning for the Always-On Generation: Strategies and Apps That Work.*

To learn more about Nicky's work, follow @nickymohan on Twitter.

To book Ryan L. Schaaf or Nicky Mohan for professional development, contact pd@SolutionTree.com.

FOREWORD

By Ian Jukes

Consider the pleasure in playing any good game. It quickly becomes evident that the built-in learning process is what makes it fun. To improve, players must constantly learn. While actively involved in a game, our brains experience the joy of struggling with, and coming to understand, new systems, concepts, and perspectives. The same principles apply to digital games and equally to entertaining games, such as *SimCity*, *World of Warcraft*, and *Angry Birds*, and serious games, like *Darfur is Dying*, *SPENT*, and *Global Conflicts: Palestine*.

In 2015, 155 million Americans played computer and video games (Entertainment Software Association, 2015). The potential for applying gaming experiences to education is astounding and practically unlimited. Using carefully designed games and simulations to accomplish specific learning goals sparks the development of highly engaged, motivated learners who enthusiastically and repeatedly engage in problem-solving activities. For example, simulations allow medical students to practice and refine surgical techniques. Games provide new pilots with the opportunity to repeatedly and safely crash while learning to fly in perilous circumstances. They also encourage students to learn the fundamental tenets of molecular biology while studying DNA at the microscopic level.

Games provide a fertile breeding ground for learning through trial and error, divergent thinking, repetition, and opportunities to lead and teach others. Well-designed video games transmit powerful and immersive story lines that compel players to work repeatedly through challenges until they achieve victory, earn a high score, ascend the leaderboard, or simply demonstrate their love of the game by playing it again.

Game On: Using Digital Games to Transform Teaching, Learning, and Assessment by Ryan L. Schaaf and Nicky Mohan examines the enormous potential of digital gaming to support learning in the modern classroom. Using the very same tools that are an everyday part of the digital generation, Schaaf and Mohan clearly outline how to leverage video games to promote compelling learning experiences, where students feel excited, engaged, and empowered.

This book is specifically designed to help educators, school leaders, curriculum designers, staff developers, trainers, and parents understand the extraordinary potential for using digital games and gameful design to provide powerful learning experiences for modern students. It provides readers with a wealth of practical ideas, implementation strategies, and research-based practices to appeal to students' learning attributes and preferences, while at the same time addressing the increased focus on academic standards and high-stakes testing.

Finally, Schaaf and Mohan include some valuable takeaways—so valuable it is like purchasing two books for the price of one. The book is absolutely packed with grade- and subject-specific learning games, numerous lesson sparks to illustrate how educators can implement digital games or simulations into classrooms, and resources and articles related to key topics.

For anyone wanting to know the *who, what, when, where, why,* and *how* for using digital games in the classroom, this is the book for you!

Introduction

The Gamer in Us All

We—the authors of this book—are gamers at heart. We enjoy playing games alone or with our loved ones in our spare time. Despite living in different countries, we have converged to write about a subject that is near and dear to us. We are both seasoned educators who have a passion for helping teachers better prepare students in the age of disruptive innovation—an age in which technology is changing the way people work, collaborate, and learn on an almost daily basis.

We work tirelessly to help prepare students for their futures, not our generation's past. We understand that today's students are different. Continuous digital bombardment has caused students to learn, communicate, and play differently than the ways their parents and today's educators did. Perhaps the perfect medium to explore these differences between generations is interactive media, such as digital games. A *digital game* is any game played on a digital device.

Indeed, digital game–based learning and *gamification* (using game-like mechanics, elements, and thinking outside of the confines of a game) have the potential to disrupt education. However, they have tremendous potential for good as well. President Barack Obama even sees this potential for gaming in education as the White House hosted the National STEM Video Game Challenge in 2012 (Evans, 2011). The challenge, which has since become an annual event, channels the passion of middle and high school students to design their own games using computer programming and technology skills. Gaming is ubiquitous; it can no

1

longer be classified as trivial, or as the late, great author Ray Bradbury labeled them, a waste of time (Lang, 2012).

To understand the impact of gaming on young people, pluck any two out of the herd and study them in their natural habitat. Take, for example, Nicky's twenty-eight-year-old son, Sherwen. He is an avid gamer who plays for sheer enjoyment. His two favorite games are *Call of Duty: Modern Warfare 3* and *FIFA* (a soccer game series). He loves the idea that he can play these games at any time, whether alone or collaboratively with others either in the same room or halfway around the world. In these games, players are known by their usernames—the only discernible identifiers are the flags that represent the players' countries of origin. Over time, Sherwen has played with gamers from the United States, Canada, Australia, South Africa, Poland, Italy, and Brazil, to name a few.

Despite coming from different cultures, time zones, and socioeconomic backgrounds, Sherwen and the other players compete and collaborate for a shared purpose. During gameplay, individual prejudices, cultural backgrounds, age, gender, and religion are nonissues. In game settings, everyone is equal. At the same time, players bring their personal knowledge, backgrounds, and individualism to the game, weaving a powerful social fabric that one could only wish might be duplicated in the real world.

Ryan's eight-year-old son, Connor, loves to play digital games on his Nintendo Wii, Xbox 360, and tablet. He also enjoys reading books, watching movies, and listening to music. However, despite his love for all of those media, the interactive nature of video games captures his interest and engages him the most. It takes a great deal of time, strategy, and grit for him to achieve goals during gameplay. Perhaps as much as it does for him to win a footrace or earn a new belt in tae kwon do. Despite expending a great deal of mental energy and time, Connor has fun—the type of fun that keeps him coming back for more, even with the constant failure involved with playing most digital games.

The members of Sherwen's and Connor's generations are fundamentally different than previous ones. They use technology constantly to learn new information and communicate with one another in large global networks known as the *digital landscape*. Digital technologies have had a profound effect on multiple generations of people; throughout this book we refer to all these generations as the *digital generation*.

Sherwen and Connor are not the only members of the digital generation who are embracing gaming. Cordell Steiner, a third-grade student from Minnesota, made a plea to teachers in a TEDx conference to use digital games in their classrooms for learning and assessment (Steiner, 2014). In this TEDx Talk, Cordell discusses how digital game–based learning provides *individualized learning*—learning focused specifically on a student's particular needs. He spotlights the attraction of digital games and the digital generation's willingness to embrace a medium in school that students enjoy at home with their friends and families. For example, when instruction calls for students to learn or review geometric angles, then they play a game that explores the concepts in a highly immersive and interactive manner with immediate feedback. Cordell also conveys the point that games allow players to fail and try again. In the traditional forms of classroom assessment, this type of failure is often "rewarded" with a low grade. If a player fails in a digital game, he or she clicks the reset button (for both the game and the learning process). In reality, digital games have a lot to teach our students and a great deal to teach educators about learning and assessment during the digital age (Schaaf, 2015).

Inside This Book

This book will provide you with a sound introduction to game-based learning and the many strategies and tools at your disposal. If you are already familiar with game-based learning, you might decide to explore the table of contents for a chapter that piques your interest or is crucial to your professional development agenda. The game lists and strategies sections provide ideas you can implement in a classroom full of learners as soon as possible. This book provides many takeaways for using digital games or gamification in the classroom for teaching, learning, and assessment.

Chapter 1, "From Entertainment to Education 3.0," provides an overall picture of the gaming industry and gaming's potential in schools. Chapter 2, "The Arcade of Education," offers a common vocabulary—terms and definitions associated with gaming in education. Chapter 3, "Learning Theory and the Attributes of the Digital Generation," illustrates the underpinning for using digital game–based learning and gamification in the classroom from respected education theorists such as Jean Piaget, James Paul Gee, and Seymour Papert, to name a few. It also provides a learning progression that supports why games are such immersive constructs for learning and how they transcend so many other forms of content and information delivery. Lastly, it introduces the general learning habits of the digital generation and shows how gaming aligns with how modern-day students learn.

Chapter 4, "How to Find and Evaluate Digital Games for Teaching, Learning, and Assessment," highlights an extensive list of potential games and gaming platforms to use with learners and also provides strategies to find digital games for instruction, along with an evaluation checklist for critiquing potential games for instruction. Chapter 5, "Lesson Design Using Digital Games," provides instructional and assessment strategies to use with students as well as directions to create small lesson starters, known as *lesson sparks*, in the classroom. Chapter 6, "Digital Gaming and Assessment," shows how games can invigorate students and set them on a course for academic success by determining where students are now, where they want to go in the future, and the path to get there. Chapter 7, "The Nine I's of Modern Learning," invites readers to contemplate how the elements of digital game–based learning align with the nine essential skills for modern learning. Chapter 8, "Universal Design for Learning With Games," examines the Universal Design for Learning (UDL) framework and how using digital games and gamification fits within this structure for student learning. Chapter 9, "Beyond Linear Presentations," allows readers to become game designers. The chapter demonstrates how to repurpose a slideshow program, such as Microsoft PowerPoint, to create a short-form digital game tailored to student needs. Chapter 10, "Takeaways," offers takeaways—powerful and extensive resources and tools.

Educators, school and instructional leaders, curriculum designers, staff developers, trainers, and parents will all witness the power of gaming in this helpful, pragmatic guide for how to find and use digital games and gameful design in the modern-day classroom.

Chapter 1

From Entertainment to Education 3.0

Show me your children's games, and I will show you the next hundred years.

—Heather Chaplin and Aaron Ruby

The gaming industry is a thriving one. It is global, diverse, and immensely popular. As of 2013, more than 1.2 billion people worldwide played some form of digital game (Takahashi, 2013). In well-established entertainment markets such as the United States and Canada, the video game industry is flexing its revenue-generating muscles. In 2011, the United States generated $17.02 billion from gaming (Bronkhorst, 2012). In 2016, the projected global revenue is estimated to be $99.6 billion a year (Newzoo, 2016); the gaming industry is attracting new users every day.

With the evolution of information and communications technologies (ICT), a new digital landscape has emerged, providing digital games with fertile ground for growth. Gaming has experienced a steady increase in revenue since the mid-2000s (Gartner, 2013), despite the struggling economy. In fact, just about every report and statistic we come across supports just how incredibly popular gaming has become in our modern-day society. If you are a bit skeptical, then let's take a look at the numbers.

In 2007, *Halo 3* generated $170 million in its first twenty-four hours of sales (Miller, 2007). In 2010, *Call of Duty: Black Ops* made a then-record $360 million in sales on the first day of its release (Schreier, 2010). In September 2013, a new media milestone was reached: *Grand Theft Auto V* made $800 million in global sales in one day, which was the biggest launch day ever for any game, movie, or album (Kamenetz, 2013). By the third day, the game topped over $1 billion in sales. Summer blockbuster movies such as *The Avengers* and *Avatar* took almost three weeks to reach that milestone.

The growth in the rate of yearly revenue for the gaming industry is almost unfathomable. In 2000, global video game sales were just shy of $50 billion. By 2008, that figure had reached over $72 billion in annual sales. In 2013, the video game industry generated over $93 billion, and the forecast for 2015 was for the gaming industry to reach sales of over $111 billion (see figure 1.1; Gartner, 2013).

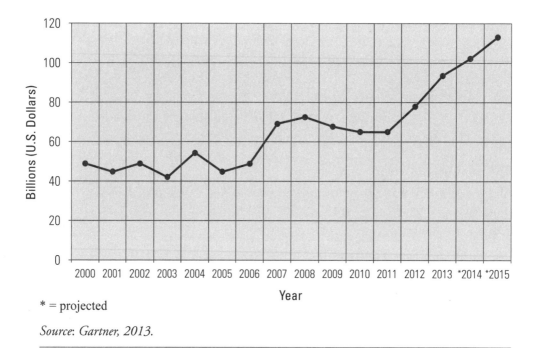

* = projected

Source: Gartner, 2013.

Figure 1.1: Global video game revenue.

Although it is challenging to locate clear, consistent data due to the different categories of video games (such as mobile, handheld, personal computer, console, and arcade), the trend is undeniable: the gaming industry is growing at a fever pitch.

These numbers show the popularity of digital games, but what about the people who play them? Traditionally, the perception of a gamer is of an adolescent boy playing games alone in a dark room. This stereotype may have been true in the past; however, with the rise of the digital age and the pervasiveness of video games, more and more nontraditional gamers are picking up the controllers and embracing this form of entertainment and socialization.

Although males participate the most in video games, according to the Entertainment Software Association (ESA, 2013), 45 percent of all game players and 46 percent of the most frequent purchasers of games are female. Amanda Lenhart, Joseph Kahne, et al. (2008) note that 99 percent of boys and 94 percent of girls indicate they have played some form of video game. Gender is no longer an isolating demographic as more and more people find engagement and excitement playing digital games.

The notion of the *lonely gamer* is an outdated concept as well. According to ESA (2013), 62 percent of gamers play with others, either in person or online. Of these gamers, over three-quarters of them play with others more than one hour per week. Players of different cultures, ethnicities, genders, age groups, and gaming ability work together to pass a level, unlock a prize, or ascend the global leaderboards. These people spend hours working with gamers they have never met face to face. Gaming technologies now allow players to connect with anyone, anywhere, and at any time.

Parents are also sharing their love of video games and gaming with their children. Sixty-five percent of American households play video games, and the average player age is thirty-five years old (ESA, 2016). Because of their love for Atari 2600, Nintendo Entertainment System (NES), and Sega Genesis, adults naturally spend time teaching their children to love playing video games:

> Gamers have grown up to have gamer kids, and families are gaming together though there is still room for growth: over one-third of parents play games with their children regularly (at least once a week) and over one half play at least once a month. 16% of kids play with parents, 40% play with friends, 17% play with their spouse or significant other and 34% play with other family members. (Galarneau, 2014)

In the United States, approximately two-thirds of households possess some form of a video game. That makes these systems even more popular than cable television (Cooper, 2011). Ninety-one percent of U.S. children between the ages of two and seventeen play video games regularly (NPD Group, 2011). As for teens, 97 percent play computer, online, portable, or console games (Lenhart, Jones, & Macgill, 2008).

The business sector is also embracing the spirit of gaming. Big corporate entities such as McDonald's, Nike, and Starbucks are using gaming elements and mechanics to bolster customer loyalty programs and sales (Chou, 2013). Have you ever played McDonald's Monopoly game, or participated in the Starbucks Rewards program, or provided a customer rating using Foursquare? If you have, then you have participated in some form of gamification. Other Fortune 500 companies such as Bank of America, Marriott, Canon, Pfizer, and Cisco Systems use digital games or simulations to train their employees in positive business practices, customer relations, and professional development (ESA, 2014; Kane & Meyers, 2010; Malhoit, 2012). Even the U.S. military, with its decades of tradition and formality, uses digital games for recruiting and training purposes (Hsu, 2010). Video games are ubiquitous in today's digital society (Schaaf, 2015). People are starting to apply gaming and its philosophies into other facets of the modern world. More and more educators are adopting gaming into their instructional programs with the goal of reaching their learners using the medium they love.

The Impact of the Digital Revolution on the Classroom

Today's children and teens, members of the always-on generation, love media. They watch television, listen to music, stream YouTube videos, interact on social media, text, tweet, and, of course, play digital games. This bombardment of digital content has created neurologically different children who have different learning experiences and preferences (Small & Vorgan, 2008). Adolescents' inherent capacity to regularly adapt to new media raises questions about the effect of one of the biggest events in modern history—the digital revolution.

This digital revolution has profoundly transformed how children and teens learn, play, and interact. The essential skills for the modern, 21st century world extend well beyond the ability to remember facts; it is critical for students to be able to logically and systematically evaluate the vast, ever-changing expanse of available data to discern signal from noise, to synthesize content, and to apply what they have learned to solve authentic challenges. In this digital age, educators must endeavor to create learning experiences that promote problem solving, critical thinking, creativity, resilience, and collaboration.

According to writer and speaker Jane McGonigal (2010), on average gamers as a whole spend more than 3 billion hours a week playing video games. How can we leverage what gamers love most—engagement and personalization—to enhance teaching, learning, and assessment? What can educators learn from this trend?

As educators, we can personalize learning and increase engagement by consistently challenging students with authentic tasks and by using digital games to create active learning opportunities that require learners to respond, innovate, create, adapt, and collaborate—not as *the* strategy but as one of a repertoire of effective learning strategies.

Gaming is not a passing fad. In some form or another, digital games have been around for generations and more and more people are adopting them globally. It would be beneficial for educators to use the same approach for learning as their students use for fun and socialization. By doing so, educators demonstrate they value student interests, and this value is an ingredient in a recipe for success in today's learning environments.

A Shift in Paradigms

How does the digital revolution fit with the numerous paradigm shifts education has experienced throughout history? These changes have been characterized as Education 1.0, Education 2.0, and Education 3.0.

Education 1.0

Education 1.0 was the first paradigm of education: the one-room schoolhouse where students received a basic education that focused primarily on the three Rs—the essential skills of reading, writing, and arithmetic—that people needed in the agricultural age (Lengel, 2013). Traditionally, only the rich or privileged received this level of education.

Education 2.0

The second shift to Education 2.0 reflects the theories of scientific management that Frederick Winslow Taylor (1911), a mechanical engineer, put forth in the latter part of the 19th century. Scientific management involves the analysis and synthesis of workflows to improve efficiencies. While Taylor's theories and principles were initially applied to factories and production lines, they were subsequently applied to education.

Scientific management emphasized standardized curricula, standardized learning progressions, standardized learning outcomes, and standardized learning time frames (Carnegie Units, also known as *seat time*) with a strong emphasis on learning the three Rs and following instruction. Students, regardless of their abilities, were expected to master the same material in a given amount of time. More than one hundred years later, the principles of scientific management continue to be an integral part of modern education theory and the foundation of Education 2.0. Teachers are the production line workers, students are the products, and the curriculum is the production line. For education to remain relevant in modern times and effectively prepare students for their individual and collective futures, educators must move beyond Education 2.0 to Education 3.0.

Education 3.0

Education 3.0 is a response to globalization, which resulted from the emergence of the digital landscape. It is an umbrella term that describes a variety of ways in which educators can infuse digital technology into learning. Educator Jeff Borden (2015) describes Education 3.0 as "a confluence of neuroscience, cognitive learning psychology, and educational technology." He feels by adding web-based, digital, or mobile technologies into the classroom it will "change what we can deliver, how we can assess, and how we might connect learners to each other, to instructors, and to content. And that connection changes . . . well, everything." What we are proposing is that instead of viewing digital tools as competition to existing teaching, learning, and assessment models, a shift to an Education 3.0 mindset should promote the use of these tools to support modern learning.

Writer Michael Horn (2014) differentiates Education 3.0 from Education 2.0 by suggesting that it goes "beyond mass education to mass-customized education through blended learning." Flexible and adaptable technology provides differentiated learning opportunities to students with diverse backgrounds and skills.

Digital game–based learning aligns closely with the Education 3.0 philosophy. Digital gaming provides educators and learners with what Willam Watson, Sunnie Watson, and Charles Reigeluth (2012) refer to as Personalized Integrated Educational Systems (PIES). They conclude that digital tools allow educators to provide customizable and personalized learning for their students. Well-designed digital games help players achieve learning goals while simultaneously supporting just-in-time learning opportunities. They provide learners with the information they need just in time to win a level, unlock a new game achievement or feature to progress through the game, or learn a new concept or skill. Learners are repeatedly tested and retested in a supportive learning environment where failure is as important as success for the learning experience. All this takes place while educators use classroom observation and player performance to determine if students have grasped the learning objective.

In the traditional teaching and learning model that supports Education 2.0, educators can sometimes unintentionally create a culture of dependency. In this culture, learners come to depend on the teacher, the textbook, or an instructional approach to obtain the necessary information to tell them whether something is right or wrong, to solve the problem for them, or to assess their level of understanding. Students may leave school with a sense that there is some external authority that is supposed to tell them what to do, as well as when and how to do it. For many students, in both schools and at home, adults are in charge. For them, teachers, parents, and other adults often make most, if not all, of the decisions for them, as students passively wait for direction.

The opposite is frequently the case when children play digital and nondigital games. Games are typically player centered rather than teacher centered, which promotes a learner-centered environment. Learner-centered environments are at the heart of the Education 3.0 philosophy. Gamers are in control of both their successes and failures. They must make careful choices to solve problems because those decisions carry potential consequences. With Education 2.0, students typically have very limited control over the learning environments they experience; while with Education 3.0, students have more say as to how the learning environments will be shaped.

Games and the experiences they provide may help the digital generation prepare for the careers of today and tomorrow. In the modern world, individuals are increasingly expected to operate in virtual environments, performing tasks such as participating in video conferences, collaborating on projects with others in different time zones, and designing materials using new digital tools. Video games, with their virtual environments, realistic scenarios, engaging formats, and customized experiences, can help prepare students for the modern world by providing them with remarkable experiences, allowing them to go places and do things that used to be unimaginable.

Schools must not only prepare students to pass mandated tests but also for life and work in the world that awaits them when they finish school. According to the National Education Association (2012), the next generation of jobs will be characterized by increased technology use and the need for extensive problem solving and complex communication.

Herbert Gerjuoy is quoted in Alvin Toffler's (1970) *Future Shock* as saying, "The illiterate of the 21st century will not be those who cannot read and write, but also those who cannot learn, unlearn, and relearn" (p. 440). In these turbulent times, we need our students to ask new questions, find new and novel solutions to problems, think critically and creatively, be imaginative and innovative, and be prepared to take risks.

A Gaming Mindset

The New Media Consortium (NMC) and the Consortium for School Networking (CoSN) collaborate each year to publish the NMC Horizon Report. The report "annually identifies and describes emerging technologies likely to have a large impact over the coming five years in every sector of education in some 65 countries around the globe" (Johnson, Becker, Estrada, & Freeman, 2014). Although the report is not meant to be a predictive tool—it's not a crystal ball with a look into the future—it does highlight potential emerging trends in technology that educators must be familiar with. Since 2010, the yearly K–12 and higher education versions of the reports have identified digital game–based learning, game-based learning, or gamification as trends that will be entering mainstream K–12 classrooms or higher education globally (Johnson, Adams, & Haywood, 2011; Johnson, Becker, Cummins, et al., 2013; Johnson et al., 2012; Johnson, Becker, Estrada, & Freeman, 2014; Johnson, Smith, Levine, & Haywood, 2010).

These trends have emerged largely because the cost to use the learning approaches is diminishing, and schools now have better infrastructure and technical support to make gaming in learning a reality. Beyond this, gaming has the overwhelming endorsement of the digital generation.

In the next chapter, we define key vocabulary associated with using games for teaching, learning, and assessment and explore how to use play as a powerful and effective approach.

Summarizing the Main Points

- With the evolution of information and communications technologies, a new digital landscape has emerged, providing digital games with fertile ground for growth.

- The gaming industry is enormous, with 1.2 billion people playing 3 billion hours of video games per week.

- The traditional idea of gamers as young boys playing solo is over. Females and males of all ages are playing digital games.

- Digital games support the development of 21st century skills that modern learners need; gameplay and online communities cultivate essential skills such as problem solving, critical thinking, creativity, resilience, and collaboration.

- Students want to have fun while they learn, but they also want learning to be challenging and relevant.

- Education 3.0 is a response to the globalization resulting from the emergence of the digital landscape. Digital game–based learning, game-based learning, play-based learning, and gamification are ideal educational approaches that are natural extensions of the Education 3.0 philosophy because they personalize and customize learning.

- The NMC Horizon Report identifies digital game–based learning, game-based learning, and gamification as potential trends to reshape learning.

Questions to Consider

1. What do you think makes video games so attractive to so many people in the world?

2. What trends have you noticed in the demographics of digital game players within your education environment?

3. Consider the skills necessary in your profession and in the globalized job market. How do digital games help cultivate these skills?

4. What does Education 3.0 mean for learning in the future? How does digital game–based learning fit into this paradigm?

Chapter 2
The Arcade of Education

If we take everything game developers have learned about optimizing human experience and organizing collaborative communities and apply it to real life, I foresee games that make us wake up in the morning and [make us] feel thrilled to start our day. I foresee games that reduce our stress at work and dramatically increase our career satisfaction. I foresee games that fix our educational systems. I foresee games that treat depression, obesity, anxiety, and attention deficit disorder.

—Jane McGonigal

The virtual worlds of gaming are an increasingly important part of kids' and adults' lives, and they are slowly making their way into education. *Play-based learning, game-based learning, digital game–based learning,* and *gamification* are gaming buzzwords in education. Many educators are not clear about what these terms mean and how they differ. In this chapter, we clarify the vocabulary and refine meaning to eliminate common misconceptions.

Play-Based Learning

Play is a powerful means for learning in child development. *Play-based learning,* whether digital or nondigital, is a strategy that uses play as the delivery method for learning new content, skills, or processes. Children cultivate remarkable skills and knowledge before they ever enter a classroom thanks to the games they play by themselves and with others. Play involves socialization, rules, self-reflection, and individual discovery. Children excel at play-based learning, which is one of the very first learning approaches they use in their cognitive development (Kennedy & Barblett, 2010). Many prominent learning philosophers and education theorists concur that play is essential for a child's cognitive development. Jean Piaget, Erik Erikson, and Lev Vygotsky all recognize the value of children using play for self-teaching (Bodrova & Leong, 2015; McLeod, 2008; Piaget, 1962). During play, children think through mental scenarios and situations. These mental exercises help develop the frontal lobes of their brains. The frontal lobe is the area of the brain associated with problem solving, emotion, planning, short-term memory, and cause and effect (Jensen, 2008). James L. Hymes, Jr. (2010) observes that play is a way for adults to determine what interests children and to assess what they understand. Play exposes children's problem-solving skills so that a parent or educator can observe how a child plans, thinks, and acts. Play also provides free, easy, try-it-yourself experiences for children where failure and experimentation teach valuable lessons. Finally, play stimulates imagination and creativity—two attributes that are highly sought after in the modern world and workplace. Best of all, play is brain friendly, and children want to engage in it (Wagner, 2008).

There is a widely held misconception that play is easy and leads to boredom, complacency, and a lack of focus. Educational visionary Seymour Papert (2002) borrowed the description *hard fun* from a student who was programming a computer using the language Logo. Although the student was having fun programming the computer, it wasn't an easy task. Papert (2002) observed that he had "no doubt that this kid called the work fun because it was hard rather than in spite of being hard." In his critically acclaimed book, *Good Video Games + Good Learning: Collected Essays on Video Games, Learning, and Literacy*, James Paul Gee (2007) makes a similar observation about the positive struggle of learning and playing challenging video games. He writes, "Good video games are hard work and deep fun. So is good learning" (p. 10). Students want to have fun while they learn, but they also want to be challenged and engaged in relevant tasks. The cause of this desire can be explained in two ways. First, the brain releases dopamine, a feel-good neurotransmitter, as a reward for conquering a challenge. Second, all children want to learn when they are emotionally invested in the learning; it's something that is hardwired into their DNA. In other words, many emotional responses may be biologically preprogrammed into humans. The love or drive to learn could be one of these preprogrammed emotions (Jensen, 2008).

Dolores A. Stegelin (2005) summarizes several attributes of play. Ideally, the individual playing should be actively engaged and have a sense of enjoyment in the experience. Play should also be open ended and allow children to physically explore different tools and materials or mentally with their own imaginations. At a young age, children enjoy engaging in activities that explore make-believe worlds. Children engage in play for its own sake—not for the explicit goal of learning.

Play-based learning also allows adults to make genuine connections with children and teens since they themselves experienced the same thrill and passion of play during their childhood and adolescence. In fact, many adults also continue to engage in some form of play throughout their lives. In addition, play is a compelling way for parents and educators to engage students in learning the essential skills for the 21st century referred to as the modern literacies (International Education Advisory Board, n.d.).

The new, modern-day literacies are the skills, knowledge, attitudes, attributes, and behaviors increasingly valued in the modern world (International Education Advisory Board, n.d.). In the digital landscape, employers are looking for workers who are experienced with problem solving, creativity, spontaneity, analytical thinking, written and oral communication, collaboration, and self-motivation—all while they are behaving in a civil and ethical manner. Digital games are incubators for developing the modern literacies—gameplay, story lines, and online communities cultivate these essential skills while simultaneously helping students learn new content.

A common form of play involves the use of games. Karl M. Kapp (2012), professor of instructional technology at Bloomsburg University, defines games in an educational context as "a system in which players engage in an abstract challenge, defined by rules, interactivity, and feedback, that results in a quantifiable outcome often eliciting an emotional response" (p. 7). Marc Prensky (2007), author of *Digital Game-Based Learning*, identified (digital) games as having rules; goals; objectives; outcomes and feedback; conflict, competition, challenge, or opposition; interaction; and representation of story. There are a marvelous variety and assortment of game types and platforms. There are digital or nondigital games, competitive or collaborative games, active or stationary games, strategy or chance-based games, complex or simple—although there is a wide array of game types, they generally have some shared elements.

- **Challenge:** The problem or scenario the player or players must overcome

- **Rules:** The structures that include boundaries players must adhere to during gameplay

- **Interactivity:** The actions or processes players experience during gameplay

- **Feedback:** The reactions players have to one another during play, including feedback for successful gameplay or consequences for mistakes

- **Conflict:** The challenge or competition between players, the game system, or rules

- **Goals or outcomes:** The desired result, such as winning or losing

Game-Based Learning

A simple definition of *game-based learning* is learning through the use of games. As a form of play-based learning, game-based learning uses the structure and experience of a game for players to learn new content or cultivate skills. Game-based learning provides a student-centered approach to instruction. Games allow teachers to step out of the spotlight and become learning guides so students can generate their own knowledge. "Students prefer participatory, collaborative learning communities in which the teacher assumes the role of facilitator or guide to help students as needed, to steer them when necessary, and to provide them with the resources and means to solve problems" (Schaaf & Mohan, 2014, p. 8). In other words, students help to create their own learning experiences.

Game-based learning is extremely fun for learners and allows them to learn from their mistakes. Researcher, speaker, and professor Steven Wheeler observes:

> Game-based learning can be so much fun it becomes addictive and as such is a really important tool for learners. Games enable learners to suspend reality and to make mistakes and learn from them. Learning from failure is a hugely important transferable skill for 21st century learning. (as cited in Tutin, 2012)

In the classroom, educators can use games to teach new material, motivate, guide independent practice and exploration, review, and assess. For example, a popular strategy is for educators to implement learning centers for students. As the educator meets with a small group for direct instruction, the other students engage in games, independent learning activities, and review tasks. With this strategy that includes game-based learning, educators can provide more attention to each student group while promoting independence and content retention in the students immersed in the centers. Of course, centers aren't the only delivery method educators can employ with their students. Before major tests, educators can use review games to help students retain information. For example, a *Jeopardy!*-like activity is a popular format educators use to help students review for tests. Game-based learning is a fun and versatile approach for educators to use with their students.

Digital Game–Based Learning

As a form of game-based learning, digital game–based learning involves the use of digital video games as teaching, learning, and assessment tools. As we have already shown in chapter 1, digital games are a popular form of entertainment. Our real-world observations attest to the connection students have with digital games. Children spend an average of thirteen hours a week playing video games (Oskin, 2012), and "seventy-two percent of children age 8 and under have used a mobile device for some media activity such as playing games, watching videos or using apps" (Rideout, 2013). The members of the always-on generation are already consuming and producing media; why not seize the opportunity and use this trend instead to flip the learning? Nicola Whitton (2010) writes:

> From an educational perspective, there is [sic] a great deal of commonalities between the characteristics of games and the characteristics of effective learning experiences. Good learning activities are intrinsically challenging—but achievable—and stretch and engage the learners through gradually increasing levels of difficulty. (p. 31)

There are numerous benefits of digital game–based learning both online and offline.

- It enhances creativity and develops problem-solving skills in the students.
- It allows students to share the joy of competition together.
- It develops students' analytical skills.

Seymour Papert, a pioneer in the field of computer science education, helped link traditional educational theories to modern practices (as cited in Blikstein,

2013). He was perhaps the first to address digital tools and their influence on children. "His awareness that children effectively think differently than adults—and that their cognitive evolution requires designing rich toolkits and environments rather than force-feeding knowledge—has set the tone for decades of research" (Blikstein, 2013). Many digital games provide these rich environments and toolkits. These virtual learning environments are some of the first places in which members of the digital generation feel the freedom to express themselves socially, creatively, and without judgment. The digital generation plays video games for fun and experiences powerful learning in their immersive virtual worlds. In these digital spaces, students have opportunities to learn through failure, take control of their actions, collaborate, and achieve goals with constant praise and reward. In many of these games and virtual worlds, there are opportunities to learn new content and explore new concepts (Schaaf, 2015).

There are a seemingly endless numbers of digital games from which to choose for classroom use. There are simulation games, serious games, logic games, commercial off-the-shelf games, mobile games, and of course, learning games. Whatever the type of game, they all encourage 21st century skills such as collaboration, persistence, practice, problem solving, and creativity.

For example, digital games do an amazing job of teaching skills and concepts. Consider the game *Angry Birds*, a strategy game in which players use a slingshot to launch birds at pigs stationed on or in various structures. The goal is to destroy all the pigs within the structures. It's a game that immediately grabs gamers' attention and can become highly addictive. *Angry Birds* addresses multiple themes and a wide range of content areas. The game addresses data collection, probability, graphing, velocity, projectile motion, vectors, parabolas, critical mass, mechanics, catapults, building design, the history of weapons, the effects of war, strategic planning, game design, feedback, shapes—the list goes on and on. Within the context of this game, we could present the following questions: Would these topics be of interest to students? Would the topics be relevant to students? Are the topics in the curriculum?

We performed a Google search for *Angry Birds and lesson plans* and got more than 1 million hits for lesson ideas. One such example is *The Physics of Angry Birds* hosted by Educade (accessed at http://educade.org/lesson_plans/physics -of-angry-birds). In this lesson, players are assessed in their knowledge and ability to apply the principles of motion and Newton's Laws of Motion during gameplay. *Angry Birds* is just one example—following are digital games that address interesting and relevant instructional topics.

- *DragonBox Algebra 5+* (http://dragonbox.com/algebra) helps students learn algebra. This game is fun to play, and students learn algebra concepts without realizing it. As players manipulate cards, they try to isolate the DragonBox on one side of the game board. Players gradually learn the operations required to isolate *x* on one side of an equation. Little by little, the cards are replaced with numbers and variables, revealing the addition, division, and multiplication operators the player has been learning throughout the gameplay.

- *Math vs. Undead: Math Workout* is an Apple and Google Play app in which students use their mathematic skills to try to stop zombies from advancing. The game mixes solving various mathematics problems with action-filled gameplay.

- *DreamBox Math* is a game available in both the Apple and Google app stores that allows students to practice mathematics on their own and at their own academic level. This tool is especially useful for differentiation when students in one classroom are at various skill levels. It offers a deeply personalized learning experience that differentiates content, pace, and sequence for the highest levels of student achievement. Players explore a robust curriculum that includes numeration, mathematical operations, problem solving, geometry, and algebra during fun gameplay.

- Disney's *Cinderella: Magical Dreams* available for the Game Boy Advance is designed to engage students through a fairy tale. Beautiful illustrations involve students, and they keep learning new things through story and pictures. Educators are able to incorporate gameplay into units involving creative writing, reading, character studies, and of course, fairy tale analysis.

Digital games have the potential to be excellent teaching, learning, and assessment tools within the educator's toolkit; however, teachers must always reach for the appropriate tool that will help students reach the targeted objectives. A list of digital games educators can use with students appears in chapter 4.

We must move beyond the negative stigma of video games to realize the power digital game–based learning can have in the classroom. Digital games are not mindless media that are a waste of time and filled with violence. We must help students unlock the potential that digital games offer and, as educators, utilize their full potential in modern learning. Teachers who are early adopters of using digital games indicate:

- Their students are more engaged—even when learning about topics that would otherwise have been uninteresting

- Their students are learning in a fun way

- They can teach both 21st century skills and content simultaneously

- They can assess student learning during the learning process

Digital game–based learning gives students a unique opportunity to learn, practice, and demonstrate their understanding of ideas in engaging ways. Players learn without feeling like they are learning or, at least, not in the traditional sense of what learning feels like. They have no fear of failing and often replay games to master their skills and abilities. And since digital games vary in format, presentation, story line, and delivery, players are treated to new experiences every time they participate.

Gamification

Gamification (often referred to as *gameful design*) is an emerging, yet largely misunderstood, field of practice that involves the use of game design and mechanics in nongaming situations. Karl Kapp (2012) provides this definition of gamification in his book *The Gamification of Learning and Instruction: Game-Based Methods and Strategies for Training and Education*: "using game-based mechanics, aesthetics, and game thinking to engage people, motivate action, promote learning, and solve problems" (p. 10). The goal of gamification in learning is to increase engagement and student enjoyment by connecting with learners and inspiring them to continue their learning. Elements of games that may motivate learners and facilitate learning through gamification include:

- **Player autonomy**—In a digital game, players have a great deal of power to make decisions and succeed or fail by their own choices. With gamification, educators look for ways of placing the decisions in learners' hands.

- **Mastery of skills**—Digital games allow players to play over and over again to master skills or review content. Repetition is a powerful learning strategy with gamification.

- **Immediate feedback**—Digital games provide both positive and negative feedback in a timely manner. This fast-paced response allows the players to adapt quickly and overcome learning challenges.

- **Collaboration**—Digital games promote teamwork and community. A combined focus on common goals replaces players' individual needs.

- **Competition**—Digital games involve conflict and challenge between individual players or teams, which can increase motivation.

- **Problem solving**—Digital games provide problems for players to solve. Problems cannot be too easy, or players will lose interest. If the game is too hard, players will become frustrated and give up.

- **Differentiated learning experiences**—Challenges within digital games can progress from simple to more difficult. They can offer the right level of challenge based on the player's current skill set or ability.

- **A compelling narrative**—Gaming immerses students in a powerful narrative. The story lines in digital games capture the player's interest to the point that he or she may imagine existing in the fantastical worlds these media create.

- **Progress data and rewards**—Digital games often provide players with data to determine how they are progressing. Badges, points, and leaderboards are a few examples of how games provide feedback to the player. Although these game mechanics are often perceived as lower-level strategies, they are easy to implement and can be combined with other strategies, such as those listed previously.

When using gamification in the classroom, educators must continually ask the following questions.

- "What are my students' interests and what would motivate them to connect with the story line?"

- "What kinds of intrinsic rewards would interest students?"

- "What game techniques, such as providing a challenge, promoting collaboration, or incorporating competition, could I use?"
- "How will I measure student success?"

When introducing gamification into your classroom, start by taking small steps. Instead of giving a percentage or grade for an assignment or project, replace the traditional marks with levels found in video games such as Novice, Expert, and Master Chief. As students complete or master classwork, they earn experience points to ascend to a new level. In the same way students advance when they play digital games, they can move to the next level only when they have mastered the previous level. For each level they achieve, learners are rewarded in some way—whether it is by receiving experience points, a special gift, or the opportunity to select the end product they will use to demonstrate their understanding. As students progress through the levels, they are challenged to use the new skills they have learned during the process. Just as with digital games, players are rewarded with powers they can use to solve problems or challenges that must be overcome in order to achieve the next level. This is empowerment. The player, in his or her quest to excel in the gamified learning environment, has taken control of his or her own learning. And if students aren't successful during their first attempt, they have the opportunity to go back to a previous level or activity and repeatedly play it for practice and reinforcement.

Gamification is an excellent fit for problem-based learning. Solving problems, whether they are real-world or simulated problems, requires students to progress through a series of stages or steps. When learning is structured as a game rather than just shared or recalled verbally, students intuitively understand the cumulative, progressive nature of the learning. They are rewarded for successfully mastering a sequence of skills. This approach allows teachers to use their imagination and creativity to develop innovative ways to reward students as they complete instructional tasks. For example, students who have collected a certain number of rewards, badges, trophies, or points are able to move on to the next academic challenge or quest.

Jane McGonigal (2011a), author of *Reality Is Broken: Why Games Make Us Better and How They Can Change the World*, observes that "A game is an opportunity to focus our energy, with relentless optimism, at something we're good at (or getting better at) and enjoy. In other words, gameplay is the direct emotional opposite of depression" (p. 28). McGonigal (2011a) introduces readers to the term *fiero*, which she describes as the rush of excitement that gamers experience when they overcome challenges. According to scientists, fiero is one of the most powerful neurochemical highs we can experience. Researchers at Stanford University say it was fiero that created the desire to leave the cave and conquer the world (as cited in McGonigal, 2011a).

To successfully gamify classrooms, teachers must ignite this powerful emotion, which will intrinsically motivate students. This motivation helps shift the responsibility of the learning from the teacher to the students. Fiero compels students to see themselves as empowered players in their education, and it helps launch them into the exciting adventure that learning can and should be. McGonigal (2011a) warns that true gamification must involve intrinsic motivation; it is not enough to simply replace a letter-based grade system with a points-based reward system. To unleash fiero and inspire intrinsic motivation, educators must incorporate the most powerful elements of digital games—challenge, a compelling narrative, player choice, constant feedback, and fun.

Gamification in Action

Educators begin with an engaging image, video, or text-based prompt and use it to craft a scenario with a story-like format that presents students with the problems, tasks, and challenges they will be encouraged to solve. Once a teacher chooses a theme or story line for the unit, he or she ensures all activities are within the framework of the story. The story can be complete fantasy, a real-world situation, or based on a simulation of an actual event. Educators can use existing games to generate ideas, or they can adapt ideas from a book, movie, or current events. Teachers can transform their classrooms to fit the theme of a unit, and students can take on real-world roles, as well as present solutions, to an authentic audience.

As an example, students can assume a mission to explore Mars. They research the planet, learn everything they can about it, and share their findings in the form of a presentation, movie, or play. Students can work in groups and take on the role of astronauts traveling to the red planet. The team can earn special mission badges for outstanding work, and students can take on the roles of team captain, science officer, and so on. Finally, student groups share what they have learned with parents, scientists, or maybe even an astronaut.

A gamified approach can support traditional subjects and content or create cross-curricular units that include two or more subject areas such as reading and science. Teachers can track learning traditionally while students track their progress using rubrics, graphs, journals, or badges. Using a narrative-based gamified teaching approach while presenting students with projects is an engaging way to create a context for learning—one that compels learners to become active participants in their learning—and it is fun, too.

Gamification With *Classcraft*

To see gamification in the classroom in action, educators should explore *Classcraft* (www.classcraft.com; see figure 2.1):

> Classcraft is a free online, educational role-playing game that teachers and students play together in the classroom. By using many of the conventions traditionally found in games today, students can level up, work in teams, and earn powers that have real-world consequences. Acting as a gamification layer around any existing curriculum, the game transforms the way a class is experienced throughout the school year. (Classcraft, 2015)

Source: Image courtesy of Classcraft Studios Inc.

Figure 2.1: *Classcraft* by Classcraft Studios.

Some of *Classcraft*'s features include:

- Interactive forums to curate and organize student assignments, resources, and discussions

- Easy-to-access leaderboards and displays

- Built-in analytics to help keep parents and administrators informed of learner performance

Classcraft immerses learners in a mythical, fairy tale realm of magic, fantasy, and adventure. The game-like interface transforms the classroom into a quest-based learning environment that teachers can easily customize to fit any grade or subject area (see figure 2.2). Students still complete their traditional assignments and learning tasks, but their performance is being measured and rewarded through the *Classcraft* platform.

Classcraft is in theory not a game; it doesn't have a centralized problem, challenge, or narrative indicative of a game. However, it is gamified; it has characters, rewards, levels, collaboration, competition, and metrics.

Source: Image courtesy of Classcraft Studios Inc.

Figure 2.2: *Classcraft* in the classroom.

Summarizing the Main Points

- Play is a powerful approach to learning. Many learning theorists, including Piaget, Erikson, Papert, and Gee, support this belief.

- Games vary in format, presentation, story line, and delivery, so players get new experiences every time they play.

- Play-based learning is a strategy that uses play as the delivery method for learning new content, skills, or processes.

- Game-based learning is learning through the use of games.

- Digital game–based learning refers to the practice of using digital games during the learning or assessment process, while gamification is the practice of using gaming elements in situations that are not games.

- Gamification is a good fit for problem-based learning. It requires students to learn and rewards them for their performance.

- Storytelling is a crucial element of using gamification in the classroom. By crafting an engaging and exciting scenario for learners to experience, educators make classroom learning a game worth playing.

- *Classcraft* is a virtual gamified environment that uses a gaming story line and mechanics to deliver content in a fun, engaging way.

Questions to Consider

1. What does play teach our children?

2. What did Seymour Papert and James Paul Gee mean when they used the term *hard or deep fun*? Consider some examples of hard fun from your experiences as a student or from your classroom.

3. Why are games such a powerful means for learning—especially in regard to childhood development?

4. What are the differences between digital game–based learning and gamification of learning?

5. How could you use gamification to promote learning in your classroom—learning that is exciting, engaging, and immersive?

Chapter 3

Learning Theory and the Attributes of the Digital Generation

To understand their world we must be willing to immerse ourselves in that world. We must embrace the new digital reality. If we can't relate, if we don't get it, we won't be able to make schools relevant to the current and future needs of the digital generation.

—Ian Jukes

To examine the impact game-based learning and gamification can have on teaching, learning, and assessment, we must first examine what some of the world's most prominent education thinkers have to say about different instructional strategies and their effects on learning.

We know that the least effective strategy for teaching is speaking (Bligh, 2000; Freeman et al., 2014). With this instructional approach, students are expected to learn by listening to the instructional content.

A more effective strategy is teaching using text and images in a visual presentation of material (Medina, 2009). This instructional approach calls on students to learn what they see. Visual information is retained in the brain more fluidly—especially for the digital generation who are growing up in a visually rich world (Jukes, Schaaf, & Mohan, 2015).

An even more effective instructional strategy than the visual presentation of material is one that combines both the audio and visual. This approach means students are listening and viewing instructional material, including activities such as watching and listening to a television program, a video, a cartoon, or a physical demonstration. By combining audio and visual elements to instructional materials, both auditory and visual learners benefit.

These three strategies are primarily passive learning activities; the learner receives information in a passive manner. With passive activities, student engagement is often difficult to evaluate because what might appear at first glance to be engagement may in fact just be entertainment or *edutainment*. These instructional strategies generally require minimal cognitive work from students. Sitting and listening means students are generally still only at the remembering, understanding, and applying levels of thought in Bloom's taxonomy (Anderson & Krathwohl, 2001), which foster only the lower levels of thinking and learning. It is important to note that these three instructional strategies encompass the majority of teaching that occurs in modern-day schools, especially as students move into high school and beyond.

Great education minds have been encouraging teachers to move beyond the traditional lecture-and-demonstration style of teaching for more than one hundred years. Researchers claim that a significant shift in mindset about teaching is necessary to foster higher-level thinking and learning. This shift starts with a move toward active-learning strategies that have students discussing the instructional material with teachers and other students, interacting with others while they are also interacting with the learning content, and so on.

As students ascend Bloom's taxonomy, they move to the higher levels of thinking involving analyzing and synthesizing information. However, merely moving to higher levels of thinking is still not the ultimate goal; instruction must shift to engaging students in real-world activities, or simulations of those activities, in multisensory learning environments. This shift allows students to begin constructing their own knowledge and learning, which moves them to the highest levels of thinking and learning: evaluating and creating. In other words, teaching strategies that foster the lowest levels of thinking and learning are teacher-centered instructional strategies where students receive information from their teachers, which results in passive learning. The teaching strategies that foster the highest levels of thinking and learning shift from passive learning to student-centered, active learning. These instructional approaches focus on facilitation so students discover things on their own. Research consistently shows that the best environments for learning involve a focus on higher-level thinking skills in active learning and multisensory or real-world situations (Lombardi, 2007; Obaid, 2013; Zohar & Dori, 2003). Figure 3.1 (page 34) is a mash-up or massive collection of learning theorists and their contributions to modern learning. The progression of thought and learning outlines the levels of thinking, how humans process new information, and the instructional materials and strategies that access these thinking skills.

As educators plan and implement lessons that access higher-order thinking skills, they must also take into account how the digital generation prefers to learn. What follows is an extensive look at the learning preferences of the always-on generation and how game-based learning (digital and nondigital) and gamified learning experiences tie into these learning attributes.

The Attributes of Digital Learners

Educators are teaching entirely different types of learners today than they did in the past. From the outside, this generation of learners looks similar to previous generations, but neurologically, they are very different. Ian Jukes, Ted McCain, and Lee Crockett (2010) examine these differences in their book *Understanding the Digital Generation: Teaching and Learning in the New Digital Landscape*. They discuss *digital bombardment and neuroplasticity*, the process of ongoing reorganization and restructuring of the brain in response to intensive inputs and constant stimulation.

They suggest that *chronic digital bombardment*—exposure to video games, television shows, movies, websites, online videos, audio clips (music and speech), podcasts, texts, tweets, slideshows, photo galleries, Instagram messages, social media content, and other forms of digital media—has permanently altered the digital generation's visual- and mental-processing abilities. As a result, students read differently, play differently, process information differently, socialize differently, communicate differently, and most important, learn differently. Jukes et al. (2010) stress that parents and educators can't ignore what's happening in the new digital landscape.

This chronic digital bombardment has transformed today's learners into digital learners. Because of this transformation, these learners have developed new learning preferences. There are nine key learning attributes of the digital generation (Jukes et al., 2015). It's important to point out that these attributes don't apply equally to every learner; factors such as culture, socioeconomics, geography, and personal experience influence learners as well.

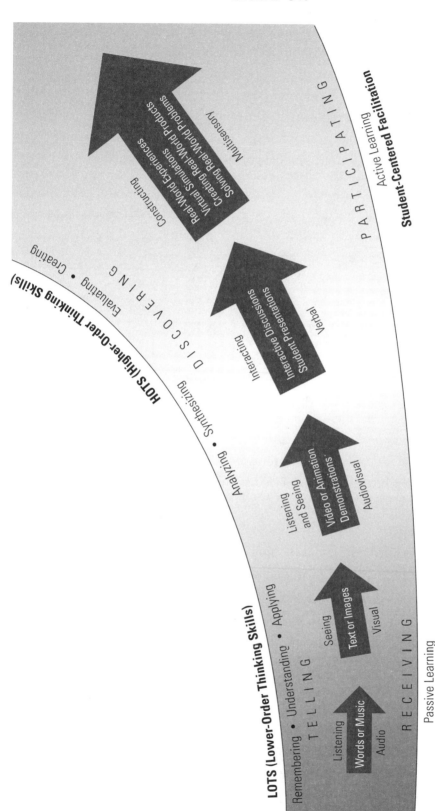

Source: Courtesy of Nicky Mohan and Ted McCain; Bloom, 1956; Dale, 1969; Dewey, 1933; Glasser, 1986; Maslow, 1943; Montessori, 1936; Piaget, 1962; Vygotsky, 1978.

Figure 3.1: Progression of thought and learning.

The Nine Learning Attributes of the Digital Generation

The nine learning attributes of the digital generation provide a starting point for teachers as they plan instruction and decide what teaching and learning strategies to incorporate into their teaching. They help educators target the most common characteristics of 21st century students and understand how the digital generation prefers to learn (Jukes et al., 2015).

1. Digital learners prefer receiving information quickly from multiple, hyperlinked digital sources.

2. Digital learners prefer parallel processing and multitasking.

3. Digital learners prefer processing pictures, sound, color, and video before they process text.

4. Digital learners prefer to network and collaborate simultaneously with many others.

5. Digital readers unconsciously read text on a page or screen in an *F*-shape or fast pattern.

6. Digital learners prefer just-in-time learning.

7. Digital learners are looking for instant gratification and immediate rewards while simultaneously looking for deferred gratification and delayed rewards.

8. Digital learners are frequently *transfluent*: their visual-spatial skills are so highly evolved that they have cultivated a complete physical interface between digital and real worlds.

9. Digital learners prefer learning that is simultaneously relevant, active, instantly useful, and fun.

The Need for Speed

Attribute 1: Digital learners prefer receiving information quickly from multiple, hyperlinked digital sources.

Digital learners prefer to learn while accessing a wealth of knowledge on the web. As they learn, the digital generation accesses a global-shared brain that stores all of the accumulated knowledge of the human race. Many digital games mimic this *fetch-and-retrieve* approach to learning new information, where learners must search, research, and alter their approaches to find what they are looking for. Digital games provide information to the player quickly to advance gameplay and the story line. They do this in a variety of ways, including with images, audio, and text, and in some cases, they do this physically using game systems such as the Xbox 360. However, information is not presented in the same manner and with the same frequency from game to game; therefore, gamers develop the ability to simultaneously interpret and process the numerous and diverse media-rich layers of games. In an age of information overload, the ability to filter information and determine its worth is a particularly valuable skill for students.

The Multitasking Mind

Attribute 2: Digital learners prefer parallel processing and multitasking.

Multitasking is something we all do every day. We walk down the street, look at our smartphones, decide what to do for dinner, talk with friends—seemingly all at the same time. Gary Small and Gigi Vorgan (2008) call this *continuous partial attention*—when people randomly switch between routine or familiar tasks, deciding which one to do next, dividing their attention.

The difference between the older generations and the digital generation is that the latter task switch much faster and more efficiently. Digital learners are simultaneously sending texts, watching videos online, listening to music, talking on smartphones, playing video games, and updating their statuses on social media. As a result, their minds must continually skim, scan, and scour in order to keep up.

Video games require players to multitask. Players must, for example, simultaneously keep track of an avatar's health, focus on the next mission, read for game information, anticipate the next course of action, and consider multiple game outcomes—all while talking to teammates or competitors online.

The Importance of Images and Sound

Attribute 3: Digital learners prefer processing pictures, sounds, color, and video before they process text.

Although text is an important feature in many video games, it is not the preferred media for gamers. Most information in video games is communicated through images and sounds. The human brain, eyes, and ears can interpret visual and audio input at incredible speeds. Video games take advantage of this biological factor and stream information using several sensory inputs simultaneously.

Despite images and audio being the dominant forms of communication within video games, text still has its place. It fills in story line gaps or provides more information if necessary.

Everyone Connected to Everything

Attribute 4: Digital learners prefer to network and collaborate simultaneously with many others.

Members of the digital generation work collaboratively to pool their insights into massive networks of knowledge and focus their efforts on the things that matter to them. They share content on YouTube, add pictures to Instagram, and hold discussions on Twitter or online forums. The gaming culture is the perfect example of this collaboration (Jukes et al., 2015).

Whether players are sitting next to one another or on opposite sides of the world, video games have evolved into highly social, virtual worlds. Gamers love to compete against one another, but games have also developed into collaborative spaces. Take for instance *Minecraft*—a game about breaking and placing virtual blocks. At first, people build structures to protect against monsters, but as the game grows, players work together to create imaginative mindscapes.

Collaboration is also an attribute of digital game–based learning. For example, *Eyewire*, from Seung Lab at MIT, is a video game developed to map the human brain. Over 100,000 people from 130 countries have already participated in this game with a purpose. Working as a global team, players map the 3-D structure of neurons, advancing neuroscience's quest to understand the human brain (Robinson, 2014). In much the same way, digital learners can work collaboratively using video games or in virtual worlds to solve problems.

Fast-Pattern Information Processing

Attribute 5: Digital readers unconsciously read text on a page or screen in an F-*shaped or fast pattern.*

Due to constant digital bombardment, members of the digital generation move their eyes in a very different way than members of past generations do when it comes to scanning a page, reading text, or searching for information.

Traditionally, readers' eyes move in what is called a *Z curve* or *Z pattern*. However, research has demonstrated that digital readers first unconsciously skim the bottom of the page and then scan the edges of the page before they start scanning the page itself for information. This is called an *F-pattern* or *fast pattern* (Nielsen, 2006). Digital learners also read and scan at incredible speeds due in part to the speed at which game screens display information.

Just-in-Time Teaching and Learning

Attribute 6: Digital learners prefer just-in-time learning.

The digital generation often follows their passions. They have the ability to acquire the necessary skills and knowledge just in time to solve a problem they encounter, just in time to settle an argument, just in time to coordinate a gathering, and just in time to do anything else they desire (using YouTube, Twitter, Snapchat, Facebook, texting, or any of the hundreds of other readily available digital tools).

Digital games incorporate *just-in-time learning*—learning that occurs when the learner needs it the most. Digital games provide players with essential information at the appropriate time during gameplay, so players can use it to win the game or accomplish their goals. Players learn through trial and error, and if they are stumped, they can seek help from the gaming community to find a solution.

Instant and Deferred Gratification

Attribute 7: Digital learners are looking for instant gratification and immediate rewards while simultaneously looking for deferred gratification and delayed rewards.

Digital culture resonates so strongly with students because it provides them with exactly what they need and want the most: both instant and deferred gratification and rewards. The digital generation seeks constant affirmation, a lot of attention, and the ability to distinguish themselves from others. They check constantly for new Snapchat messages, likes on Facebook, comments on their

YouTube videos, and retweets on Twitter. Digital technology, and social media in particular, provide constant gratification and reward. With video games, the user is rewarded if he or she puts in the hours and masters the game by getting to the next level, winning the game, achieving a place on the high score list, or simply gaining a skill that his or her peers respect.

Regardless of how effective a teacher is, he or she can't always offer instant gratification and reward to every student, every minute, every day. Digital technologies like video games are designed to keep players enticed and motivated in both the short and long term.

Transfluency

Attribute 8: Many digital learners are frequently transfluent*: their visual-spatial skills are so highly evolved that they have cultivated a complete physical interface between digital and real worlds.*

Members of the digital generation have become completely comfortable using a wide range of media and can seamlessly shift between digital and nondigital worlds. For them, the new digital landscape is a natural, transparent space that they have fully integrated into their lives. It does not exist in isolation from the physical world. In fact, it has become so internalized that many digital learners live a hybrid existence that seamlessly integrates communication, information, and entertainment with social media to create virtual worlds that past generations often struggle to understand.

This hybridity is possible because many digital learners are transfluent: they can switch back and forth between the real world and the digital world with ease, and they can seamlessly fit the two worlds together through the use of their digital devices.

Digital games immerse players in virtual worlds. Transfluency allows players to effortlessly shift from one world to the other, learning new content and skills in the digital world that they can carry over to nondigital environments. As an example, students can learn to drive using a digital driving simulator, then transfer their newly developed driving skills to the real world.

Relevant, Active, Useful, and Fun Learning

Attribute 9: Digital learners prefer learning that is simultaneously relevant, active, instantly useful, and fun.

Outside of school, the digital generation is *hyperconnected*—constantly linked to others to form a global intelligence. Digital learners are immersed in virtual environments and exist in a participatory culture that allows them to interact not only with local friends but also simultaneously with people who live on the other side of the world. Not long ago, this type of instant communication was impossible.

The digital generation is highly social, just not social in the same way as previous generations. Digital learners live at least part of the time in digital worlds they've created for themselves, staying constantly connected to everyone and everything.

In their virtual environments, they can create and control. They are users. They are consumers. They are producers. They are active. There is excitement, novelty, risk, and connection to peers. The virtual world is somewhere they can turn for advice and information. They observe, inquire, participate, discuss, argue, play, critique, and investigate. Digital technologies engage the digital generation in ways that are relevant to learners' lives, allowing them to learn by doing as they experiment with new social and cultural experiences.

Game-Based Learning and the Digital Generation

These attributes extend beyond the use of digital game–based and gameful learning. As educators plan and implement instruction, they must use these attributes to target how digital learners prefer to learn. Digital game–based learning and gamification challenge traditional mindsets in teaching that situate students as passive recipients in the knowledge-sharing process.

Because digital games are highly visual, they appeal to the digital generation, and because these digital games are interactive, they make learning enjoyable and engaging. In this time of change in the education system, it is imperative that educators make the process of learning informative, engaging, and captivating. Using games can be a very valuable means to teach complex concepts and content and assess student learning simultaneously.

Traditional testing scenarios tend to activate competitive skills and anxiety among students (Hembree, 2012). However, using games tends to evoke completely different responses. Competition is fun and gamers share their knowledge with their peers. We want our students to experience the same kind of fun and enjoyment on their learning journeys.

The interactivity of digital games helps teachers make the move to a more student-centered learning environment. Using this approach will bring excitement into the classroom by involving students in the learning and decision-making process. Student-centered learning gives learners the opportunity to evaluate their thinking, solve problems, and analyze information just in time (to win a level, answer the question correctly, and unlock the next challenge).

Through the use of digital games for teaching, learning, and assessment, students are active participants in the learning process. They are interacting, discussing, sharing, constructing, making decisions, evaluating, giving and receiving feedback, and collaborating, not just listening. They are demonstrating all those critical modern learning skills that they must know and develop to succeed in the 21st century world outside of school.

Digital games allow learners to explore for themselves. They have immersive story lines, where decision making is unavoidable, and thereby reinforce higher-order thinking skills. Educators can use games as the medium to help their students become independent problem solvers and lifelong learners. Because students experience success and receive immediate feedback and rewards, they keep coming back for more. They are willing to persevere to move on to the next level or stage.

Summarizing the Main Points

- During our time of great technological change, educators must make broad changes in their teaching, learning, and assessment methodologies.

- Learning theorists such as Dewey, Montessori, Piaget, Bloom, and Maslow help educators understand the need to change teaching practices.

- Learning through audio and visual modalities is common in schools. Unfortunately, this kind of instruction fosters lower-order thinking and learning.

- The ultimate goal is to shift instruction to engage students in real-world activities, or simulations of those activities in multisensory learning environments. By doing this, students begin constructing their own knowledge.

- The digital generation experiences chronic digital bombardment—pervasive digital exposure that has permanently altered learners' visual and mental processing abilities and caused them to develop new learning preferences.

- There are nine key learning attributes of the digital generation.

- Digital games and game-based learning approaches cater to the nine learning attributes of the digital generation.

- Digital games are highly visual, which appeals to the digital generation. Because these digital games are interactive, it makes learning interesting and engaging, while simultaneously involving higher-order thinking skills.

- Educators can use games as a medium to help their students become independent problem solvers and lifelong learners.

Questions to Consider

1. Why do you think change is often so difficult for educators?

2. According to Mohan and McCain's progression of thought and learning (see figure 3.1, page 34), what instructional strategies and approaches access higher-order thinking skills?

3. How will understanding and using the nine learning attributes of the digital generation help transform your teaching practices?

4. How do you think utilizing the devices and technologies the digital generation is accustomed to using will help establish a connection to the classroom?

5. Are any of the nine attributes more important, in your opinion?

6. Can you think of any instructional strategies, apps, digital tools, or services that would align with a particular attribute?

7. How do digital game–based learning and gamification perpetuate higher-order thinking skills?

8. Why is some competition just as healthy as collaboration? How does gaming help cultivate the competitive spirit?

Chapter 4

How to Find and Evaluate Digital Games for Teaching, Learning, and Assessment

> *If a child can't learn the way we teach, maybe we should teach the way they learn.*
>
> —Ignacio Estrada

The evolution of information and communication technologies has created an expansive digital landscape with amazing resources for educators. Nowadays, almost anyone can create a digital game—from kids and small app developers all the way up to giant gaming companies. Game producers, both big and small, are taking notice of how powerful digital games can be for learners at home and in classrooms.

What educators and parents struggle with is where to find high-quality games. At present, the digital learning game market relies too heavily on word of mouth or biased advertisements from game producers. It is imperative for educators, parents, and even learners themselves to know where to find good learning games in a vast sea of available game titles and determine if these games are effective tools for learning.

Playing Serious Games

In the past, digital games were adopted as learning tools infrequently in only a small number of classrooms and used as just a content-delivery platform (Provenzo, 1991). However, the meteoric rise in gaming's mainstream popularity and appeal has compelled educators to take a second look at the use of digital games as virtual environments for deep, fun, and engaging learning. The video game industry has succeeded in creating a media format that is both immersive and entertaining. Educators and society in general must rethink how we view games because many of them can be powerful resources for teaching and learning. What if, instead of being just entertaining, a game served another purpose? What if it promoted social awareness or responsibility? What if it encouraged altruistic or charitable acts? What if it was designed to disperse content in an interactive way that immersed students in learning?

Consider how other media formats have already experienced a transformation in purpose in education. Take, for instance, video. For decades, the main purpose of video (movies and television) was to entertain viewers. However, educational shows emerged (such as *Sesame Street* and *Reading Rainbow*) that both entertained and, more important, educated young viewers, creating what some might call *edutainment*. Today's educators often use DVDs and streaming video to aid in instruction.

Serious games started to surface in the early 2000s. According to Alex Hort-Francis (2014), *serious games* are "games designed for a primary purpose other than entertainment. They involve the use of electronic games technologies and methodologies and are meant to take on real-world problems." Although it doesn't have to be a serious game for learning to happen, serious games have a great deal of success in teaching learners (Wouters, van der Spek, & van Oostendorp, n.d.) because they are designed with a specific learning objective, such as developing social awareness, receiving training, or experiencing digital storytelling.

With serious games, education and training are the main purposes; entertainment may be a byproduct. Serious games encourage learners to take an active role in their learning while receiving immediate feedback. Learners can then reflect on the decisions they've made while playing the game and apply what they have learned in school or in their lives.

Serious games are rich in real-world scenarios and opportunities for higher-order thinking skills application. For example, consider games in which:

> Players learn biology by working as a surgeon, history by writing as a journalist, mathematics by designing buildings as an architect or engineer, geography by fighting as a soldier, or French by opening a restaurant. . . . These players learn by inhabiting virtual worlds based on the way surgeons, journalists, architects, soldiers, and restaurateurs develop their epistemic frames. (Shaffer, Squire, Halverson, & Gee, 2005, p. 108)

Serious games have the ability to change player perspectives and provide safe avenues for players to take risks while at the same time learn new information and skills. There is also a wide variety of subject matter covered in these games. What follows are several examples of serious games to demonstrate what's available for educators and explain what the games teach players.

Free Rice (http://freerice.com) is a nonprofit game where users answer questions in subjects like the humanities, mathematics, geography, chemistry, English, and foreign languages. The game uses a custom database containing questions that vary in difficulty. There are levels for beginners all the way up to experts. In between are levels suitable for students of all ages, and adults as well. *Free Rice* automatically adjusts to the player's level. It starts with questions of increasing difficulty and then, based on how the player does, assigns an approximate starting point. The player determines a more exact level as he or she plays. When players answer a question correctly, the United Nations World Food Programme donates ten grains of rice to people in need around the world. The game, though very simple in design, promotes altruism and charity. It also perpetuates a larger world view of the struggles people still face in developing countries.

At the date of this publication, *Free Rice* has distributed over ninety-five billion grains of rice (World Food Programme, n.d.) for refugees, to aid school lunch programs, to help after natural disasters, and so on, to such places as:

- Cambodia
- Bangladesh
- Bhutan
- Haiti
- Myanmar
- Nepal
- Uganda

Gameplay that serves a powerful purpose ties back to the final learning attribute of digital learners—they prefer learning that is simultaneously relevant, active, instantly useful, and fun. The game is relevant and useful because it is helping others. And since this help is offered in the context of a game, it is fun.

Darfur is Dying (www.darfurisdying.com) provides a window into the experiences of the 2.5 million refugees in the Darfur region of Sudan. Players must keep their refugee camp functioning in the face of possible attack by Janjaweed militias.

Player tasks include:

- Collecting water—Players must forage for water while avoiding militants.

- Obtaining food—Players must collect water from pumps and take it to the vegetable gardens. Once the gardens grow, players must return to harvest the crops.

- Building shelters—Players deliver water to dirt plots to make bricks and other materials necessary for rebuilding structures that have been destroyed.

- Staying healthy—Players must also visit a clinic for the sick when new medical and food supplies arrive.

The goal is to maintain a functioning camp for seven days. The threat meter keeps a constant measure of the possibility of an attack, which will eliminate the food and water supply, destroy structures, and affect the health of the camp.

Players can also uncover ways to get involved to help stop this human rights and humanitarian crisis by clicking on the red Take Action button embedded throughout the game. The content of the game can be quite graphic, so please exercise caution when presenting this content to players.

PeaceMaker (www.peacemakergame.com) is a web-based game inspired by real events in the Israeli–Palestinian conflict. Players take on the role of a leader with a mission to bring peace to the region before his or her term in office ends. Exploring both sides of the conflict, *PeaceMaker* allows players to assume the role of the Israeli prime minister or the Palestinian president. The game also uses real news footage and images (rated PG-13 for grades 7–12).

There are three difficulty levels to choose from: calm, tense, and violent. The game design makes the following assumptions:

- Everyone can make a difference!
- The winning state is the two state solution; the other side wants peace, too.
- Players must take small concrete steps—not make grandiose plans.
- Perfection is the enemy of the possible!

The game also includes a blog players can access.

FloodSim (http://playgen.com/play/floodsim) puts the player in control of flood policy in the United Kingdom for three years. (See figure 4.1, page 50.) It is an accessible online simulation that helps raise public awareness of issues around flood policy and provides feedback to insurers and policymakers about public attitudes toward different flood protection options. Players must decide how much money to spend on flood defenses, where to build houses, and how to keep citizens informed. But, as in real life, money is limited. The player must analyze flood risks in different regions against the potential impact on the local economy and population. The game brings to life the complexities of the issues policymakers struggle with in real life.

Key messages and themes include:

- Money management
- Impact of flooding on the economy and local populations
- Understanding governmental policy and how to take action
- How to make better informed decisions by crowdsourcing the opinions of citizens and stakeholders

In *EteRNA* (www.eternagame.org), players construct ribonucleic acid (RNA) sequences using matching and stacking gameplay similar to popular games such as *Candy Crush*. Developed by Stanford University and Carnegie Mellon University scientists, *EteRNA* allows players to create new RNA sequences that have a chance of being produced in a real-world chemistry lab. Players are introduced to the essential vocabulary and concepts associated with molecular biology as they make new RNA strands and potentially create new medicines to cure diseases.

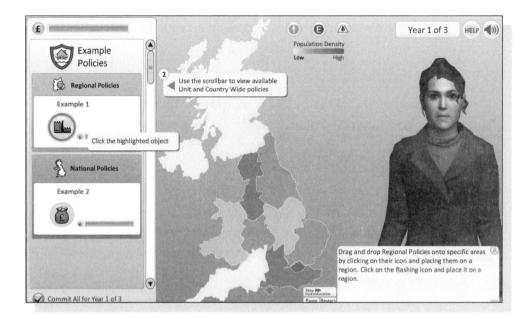

Source: Courtesy of Playgen. © 2016 Playgen.

Figure 4.1: *FloodSim* gameplay.

These examples of serious games are only a few of the ever-growing number available to educators. One of the real challenges for educators, parents, and learners is to know where to look for games and how they can be used both inside and outside of school. Serious games are one game type to consider adapting for learning experiences. However, there are dozens of other types of games to consider using with learners. What follows is a description of the numerous game platforms, genres, and resources that are available for both educators and learners to explore.

Playing Browser-Based Games

There are tens of thousands of digital learning games available online at this very second. Educators can perform a simple Google search for content-specific games to infuse into their lessons. For instance, imagine a group of science students learning about life cycles. A teacher simply searches *interactive life cycle games for kids* to find hundreds of potential games.

Since many U.S. schools already have various digital devices, such as computers and iPads, browser-based games are the easiest to add to existing lessons. If students have access to their own digital devices in the classroom, then they can play concurrently in a one-to-one computing environment. If there are more students than computer stations, teachers can employ collaborative gaming experiences with students. In other words, students play in teams using one device. Educators can also create their own learning or teaching centers in order to use gaming in the classroom. They can set up learning activities around the room and have students rotate through the stations to experience each of them. During the rotation, learners can visit a station that hosts a digital learning game.

The ideal classroom situation for using digital learning games is a one-to-one computing environment. The challenge in using this strategy is that teachers may let students play freely without regularly observing their progress, checking to see if students are struggling or monitoring them to determine whether a certain game is too easy or difficult. If there is no consistent instructional guidance or student accountability, there is the risk that the games may become little more than digital busywork. Teachers can avoid this by being sure to monitor student progress. They can perform these checks by making classroom observations, assigning gaming partners, or having students complete an exit ticket or self-evaluation.

Digital Learning Game Hubs

Large online collections of browser-based digital learning games are often referred to as *game hubs*. These sites house many different types of digital games tailored to specific content areas and ages. Table 4.1 is an extensive list of online learning game hubs for educators to use as resources for technology learning centers or as support or for extra practice at home.

Table 4.1: Game Hubs

Game Hub	Website
ABCYa.com (grades preK–5)	www.abcya.com
Arcademic Skill Builders (grades 1–6)	www.arcademics.com
BrainPOP (grades K–12)	www.brainpop.com/games
Disney Games (all ages)	http://games.disney.com
Fun4theBrain (grades K–12)	www.fun4thebrain.com
Funbrain (grades K–9)	www.funbrain.com
Games for Change (all ages)	www.gamesforchange.org
GoGo Math Games (grades K–8)	www.gogomathgames.com

continued →

Game Hub	Website
iCivics (grades 3–12)	www.icivics.org/games
NCTM Illuminations (grades 3–8)	http://illuminations.nctm.org/Games-Puzzles.aspx
Shodor Interactivate (grades 3–12)	www.shodor.org/interactivate
IXL (grades preK–12)	www.ixl.com
JumpStart (all ages)	www.jumpstart.com
KidsGamesHQ (all ages)	http://kidsgameshq.com
Knowledge Adventure (grades preK–6)	www.knowledgeadventure.com
Learn4Good (grades preK–6)	www.learn4good.com/games/index.htm
Learning Games for Kids (grades K–12)	www.learninggamesforkids.com
Math Playground (grades 1–6)	www.mathplayground.com
Mr. Nussbaum (grades preK–6)	http://mrnussbaum.com
Nickelodeon (grades preK–6)	www.nick.com/games
Nobelprize.org (grades 9–12, higher education)	www.nobelprize.org/educational
PBS KIDS (grades preK–6)	http://pbskids.org/games
Penn State's Educational Gaming Commons (EGC) Live (grades 9–12, higher education)	http://play.gaming.psu.edu
Poptropica (grades 3–6)	www.poptropica.com
PowerMyLearning (grades K–12)	http://powermylearning.org
PrimaryGames (grades preK–6)	www.primarygames.com
Prongo (grades preK–7)	www.prongo.com/games
Sheppard Software (grades preK–7)	www.sheppardsoftware.com
Smarty Games (grades preK–4)	www.smartygames.com
SoftSchools.com (grades preK–12)	www.softschools.com
Sprout (grades preK–3)	www.sproutonline.com/games
The STACKS (grades preK–6)	www.scholastic.com/kids/stacks/games
Sumdog (grades K–8)	www.sumdog.com

Steam

Steam (http://store.steampowered.com) is an online-gaming platform that hosts a massive online catalog of over 4,500 games for PC, Mac, and Linux-based computers, mobile devices, and even smart televisions. With over 125 million users, Steam has evolved into a haven for online social gaming. Gamers can play, hold online discussions, develop tutorials, and share game ratings through a vibrant participatory community platform.

Games like *Kerbal Space Program* allow players to use engineering to create their own spacecraft and test its flight potential. Players can learn about genetics when they experiment with plants in *Crazy Plant Shop*. Similar to browser-based games, Steam delivers games to the user through the web; players must have access to a computer with the Internet to use the platform.

Playing Games Through Apps

The eruption of application, or app, markets has created a digital gold mine of potential games for learners. The two major app markets are Apple's App Store and Google Play. The App Store serves users on Apple's operating system (iOS) devices, such as the iPhone and iPad. Google Play supplies apps to smartphones and tablets using an Android platform. Apple's App Store and Google Play alone have a combined 2.9 million available apps for download (Statistica, 2015b).

The most popular types of apps in these stores are games or educational apps (Statistica, 2015b). In fact, the Apple App Store curates useful games and apps into an Education section featured on its main page for easy review and selection.

Smartphones and tablets, the devises on which apps work, have become common household items; children play on tablets in restaurants and use them on car rides or while sitting on the couch on a rainy day. Schools are increasingly embracing tablets as teaching and learning tools as well. According to Tim Cook, the CEO of Apple, his company has captured 95 percent of the tablet market in schools (Kovach, 2014), and about one-third of U.S. students use a school-issued mobile device (Nagel, 2014). Despite many school success stories such as Brockport Central School District (Netop, 2013) in New York and Franklin Academy High School (Walsh, 2014) in North Carolina where iPad one-to-one computing initiatives showed success in student achievement and performance, some programs are doomed to fail. The Los Angeles Unified School District's $1.3 billion one-to-one iPad initiative, which started in 2013, was suspended in 2015 due to unethical bidding practices, technical issues, student hacking, and the lack of a fair and impartial pilot program to compare the iPad's efficacy with other devices (Jacobs, 2014).

Successfully implementing a tablet initiative requires careful planning, collaboration, support, and professional development. Many schools are adopting tablet or bring your own device (BYOD) initiatives to infuse more technology into classrooms to prepare their students for college and future careers. With their long battery life, wireless Internet access, and tactile interface, tablets have provided an intriguing technological solution for many school systems around the world.

Many middle and high school students have their own smartphones. With access to the same app markets as tablets, smartphones are another viable choice for gaming in the classroom. Teachers can take advantage of the powerful computers students carry in their pockets—the same devices students prefer to use when not in school.

Following are some gaming apps that educators can incorporate into instruction.

Angry Birds

Subjects: Mathematics and science
Ages: All

Angry Birds (www.rovio.com) is the megahit game that launched a feathery empire; it uses birds as projectiles to defeat evil pigs. The game has become so popular (over 2 billion downloads) that Rovio has released several spin off games including *Angry Birds Space*, *Angry Birds Rio*, and *Angry Birds Star Wars* (Robertson, 2014). Despite its rather silly nature, *Angry Birds* is filled with opportunities for classroom application. The game explores Newtonian physics, parabola, trajectory, cause and effect, trial and error, and strategy, to name a few.

Bridge Constructor

Subjects: Engineering, science, and mathematics
Ages: Four and up

In *Bridge Constructor* (http://bridgeconstructor.com), which is available on Google Play, Apple's App Store, and the Windows Phone Store, players become bridge engineers and architects in a building-simulation game. Players create and design their own bridges and then watch cars and trucks either pass over them safely or fall and crash (if the bridge is not well built). Players' imaginations are limited only by in-game budget constraints.

Math Duel: 2 Player Math Game

Subject: Mathematics

Ages: Seven and up

Math Duel: 2 Player Math Game (http://bit.ly/1zR1Y62) is a fun educational game where two players compete against each other mathematically. This game helps students ages seven and up practice their basic mathematics facts (addition, subtraction, multiplication, and division) in a fun and competitive way.

Powers of Minus Ten

Subjects: Science and mathematics

Ages: Four and up

Powers of Minus Ten (http://powersofminusten.com) is available on the App Store and Google Play. It lets students explore human cells and molecules while conceptualizing magnitude. They can discover some of the basic concepts in biology and learn about the structures of key cells, proteins, and molecules found in the human body. The iPad version of *Powers of Minus Ten* includes instructional minigames.

The Oregon Trail: American Settler

Subjects: Social Studies, science, and mathematics

Ages: Four and up

The Oregon Trail: American Settler (http://apple.co/2eoQ2sv and http://bit .ly/1F879o8) is a historical simulation game that allows players to build a town during the United States' westward expansion. Players must construct buildings, plant crops, raise livestock, generate revenue, and solve historically accurate problems of the era. This game explores key concepts in history, civics, economics, mathematics, and social studies. The game is available on Apple's App Store and Google Play.

The Sandbox

Subjects: Social Studies, science, and mathematics

Ages: Four and up

The Sandbox (www.thesandboxgame.com) is a game based entirely on the laws of physics (for example, gravity, fluid dynamics, and inertia). Players craft their own virtual worlds by exploring over two hundred different resources, such as water, soil, lightning, lava, sand, and glass in the form of pixels. There are also more complex elements to the game, which include humans, zombies, robots, dinosaurs, monuments, wildlife, animals, trees, gems, vehicles, sensors, explosives, and contraptions. The game is available on Apple's App Store, Mac App Store, Google Play, Steam, and Amazon.

ThinkerToy: Shapes

Subject: Mathematics
Ages: Four and up

ThinkerToy: Shapes (http://thinkertoy.com), which is available on Apple's App Store, allows players to create objects using tangrams. The app comes bundled with nearly one hundred picture puzzles for players to produce and is a fun way to explore geometry while being creative.

VocabularySpellingCity

Subjects: Spelling, reading, and language arts
Ages: Four and up

VocabularySpellingCity (www.spellingcity.com/app) is an award-winning learning tool for vocabulary, spelling, writing, and language arts. The app offers dozens of learning games with the option for teachers to track student performance and generate vocabulary lists.

With thousands of games spread across numerous mobile platforms, app markets are extraordinary sources for potential games for tablets and smartphones. Each game has a downloadable game summary, content-rating system, and user reviews, making it possible to research a game to determine if it would be a good choice for the classroom.

As always, parents and educators must be wary of game developers and their claims of boosting academic achievement. The app markets are filled with entrepreneurs trying to sell products and make money. These app designers are not typically experts in curriculum or instruction. Ultimately, teachers, curriculum developers, and parents must judge if a game or app is worthy to download and use with students.

Playing Personal Computer Games

Although mobile technologies are a trend in education, desktop computers are still a staple for many schools. Personal computers (PCs) have powerful processors, use bigger screens, are easier to use in keyboarding instruction, and promote better ergonomic practices.

Software games such as *Reader Rabbit*, *SimCity*, and *Civilization* have found some success in school computer labs as instruction for students during downtime. Despite some success with these programs, real learning occurs when the gameplay is connected to activities outside of the confines of the game. For example, learners playing *Civilization* while they learn about Ancient Greece, the Roman Empire, or France during the time of Napoleon I learn how empires are created, maintained, and lost—a common theme throughout history. *Civilization* helps players explore historical themes in politics, government structure, and global conflict.

Table 4.2 is a listing of potential PC learning games to incorporate into instruction. The list includes the game's title, the subject area, the approximate grade levels, and a reference link for educators to use while evaluating the game for potential use with learners.

Table 4.2: PC Learning Game List

Games	Subjects	Grade Level	Website
Bookworm	Reading	Grades 3–7	www.popcap.com/bookworm
Brainiversity	Mathematics, problem solving, logic	Grades 2 and up	www.brainiversity.com/About.html
Crazy Machines II	Science, engineering	Grades 2 and up	www.crazymachinesgame.com
FutureU	NA/SAT preparation	Grades 9 and up	www.aspyr.com/games/futureu-the-prep-game-for-sat
Hearing Music	Music	Everyone	http://bit.ly/2dSXeh1
Gone Home	Language arts	Grades 9 and up	https://fullbright.company/gonehome
MySims	Social studies, civics	Grades 2 and up	www.ea.com/mysims

continued →

Games	Subjects	Grade Level	Website
Spore	Science, biology	Grades 5 and up	www.ea.com/spore
World of Zoo	Mathematics, science	Everyone	http://store.steampowered.com/app/43100

Playing Console Games

Gaming consoles are possibly the last platform teachers would consider using as learning tools for their students to access highly interactive virtual learning environments. However, there are educators who are exploring the possibility of using consoles with their learners. In *Level Up Learning: A National Survey on Teaching With Digital Games*, Lori Takeuchi and Sarah Vaala (2014) show that about 13 percent of students access digital games using a game console or hand-held gaming device in schools—a significant number to say the least. Teachers are repurposing gaming consoles and using them as instructional workstations rather than as entertainment systems. With careful consideration, gaming consoles and devices have a lot of potential for classroom learning applications. Many learners have these same gaming consoles at home, so they already know how to use them.

Meghan Hearn and Matthew Winner (2013) demonstrate the hidden potential that a Nintendo Wii offers to learners. In their book *Teach Math With the Wii: Engage Your K–7 Students Through Gaming Technology*, they introduce parents and educators to embedded mathematics within Wii console games. They provide a comprehensive list of potential games to use with students, lesson sparks for teachers to use with their students, and integration strategies to help teachers facilitate these new learning experiences in classrooms.

Wii Sports consists of bowling, golf, baseball, tennis, and boxing. Many sports games are filled with embedded mathematical concepts. Imagine a classroom with a Wii connected to an LCD projector and speakers, two Wii Remotes, and the *Wii Sports* game. As two students play golf, the teacher asks students to find the difference between each student's turn to see who drove the ball the farthest (subtraction), or students can calculate how far they drove the golf ball during each turn (addition). In bowling, students can practice their addition of basic mathematics, such as finding as many combinations as they can that add up to ten; or they can calculate by how much a student won by subtracting the final scores. In essence, game data, such as numbers, meters, graphs, rankings, currency, and time are valuable sources of embedded mathematics. Teachers can exploit the hidden value of embedded curricular concepts during learning.

The always-changing nature of gaming technologies means that new systems regularly replace older ones. Thus, old systems and their games become available at a reduced price. Students and parents might also donate older consoles that they have replaced for use in the classroom.

There are also portable game consoles such as Sony's PlayStation Portable (PSP), the Nintendo DS, and LeapFrog's Leapster. These portable consoles provide players with hands-on gameplay for a much smaller price. They also do not require a television, screen, or speakers to provide the video and audio interface. At an average of one-third the cost of a traditional gaming system, portable consoles have serious potential for students, especially younger students. LeapFrog has a wide variety of educational games such as *Letter Factory*, *Animal Genius*, or *Jake and the Never Land Pirates* for young players. The Nintendo DS has gaming titles such as *Learn Math*, *Digging for Dinosaurs*, *Reader Rabbit: Kindergarten*, and *Sesame Street: Elmo's A-to-Zoo Adventure* for parents and educators to consider. In fact, the Nintendo DS was integrated into Japanese museums and schools in 2010 by iconic Nintendo game designer Shigeru Miyamoto (Dybwad, 2010).

Now that you've learned about serious games and accessing games on different media, we'll discuss finding, evaluating, integrating, and piloting games.

Finding Games

Finding high-quality learning games is a task that requires research, time, patience, and a bit of luck. It's a process. The first step is to understand how students will play the game. For example, if students do not have portable game consoles, then games designed for these types of devices are not a possibility. Educators must think of the devices and technology infrastructure they have access to. For instance, if a teacher has access to a cart filled with iPads, then he or she must find games that the device supports. Next, consider how learners will access the game. Will each student have access to a device for a whole-class gaming experience, or will students need to break into small groups to share a device for gameplay? To illustrate this point, if student groups are required to create replicas of famous buildings around the world using *Minecraft*, then they must have access to enough devices and a shared virtual space to create their buildings. Or, if students are required to practice their mathematics facts using *Arcademic Skill Builders* in a certain time frame, then they must have individual access to the game on a device. Answering these questions will provide educators with a better understanding of how to implement a lesson or activity using the available technology at hand.

Evaluating and Integrating Games

Not all digital games are created equal. Although the gaming market is saturated with potential titles, many fall short in quality or academic rigor. After all, game developers aren't educators. According to writer Jordan Shapiro and colleagues, "The best learning games teach in the same way good teachers teach: They don't trick students into being interested, they help students find genuine excitement in learning a subject" (Shapiro, Tekinbas, Schwartz, & Darvasi, 2014, p. 20). Educators must always begin with curriculum sources. For many educators, this involves consulting their district or state curriculums—or the Common Core State Standards for English language arts and mathematics (National Governors Association Center for Best Practices & Council of Chief State School Officers [NGA & CCSSO], 2010b, 2010c). From the standards, educators create a learning objective for their students and identify the tools and resources essential to help them achieve these objectives. Finally, they consider what instructional and assessment strategies to employ to reach all learners. This approach also works when choosing digital learning games; however, it will probably be easier to start with selecting a potential game and then structuring learning experiences around it. This is not a common practice when crafting lesson plans. In essence, when using a digital game during instruction, an instructional resource (the game) is dictating which academic standard an educator must teach their students. Typically, educators select their standards first, then prepare materials and strategies to help their students master the lesson objectives. Planning outward in this way may seem nonsensical to educators, but it makes sense with digital games, as they were not always constructed with the purpose of being used in a classroom lesson. Either way, teachers must consider what they are teaching students and find a game that aligns with the desired student learning outcomes.

The second consideration for evaluating and ultimately incorporating a digital game into instruction is to identify if the game is a testing game, teaching game, or both. Karl Kapp (2013), an instructional technology professor at Bloomsburg University and a pioneer in the field of using digital games and gamification in learning, describes these two types of games:

> Testing games are games where the learner already needs to know the information to be successful. The focus of the game is not to apply knowledge but rather to recall knowledge. . . . If you want to test knowledge, testing games are fine but do not expect learning to occur. . . . Teaching games, on the other hand, do not test knowledge; they impart knowledge. This is accomplished through a series of activities within the game that teaches the learner what he or she needs to do.

As digital games continue to evolve, these two classifications of testing and teaching games begin to merge, because more and more games are becoming both—they first teach the learner, and then they test or assess the learner's understanding of the content or skills the player learns or develops.

For example, an ideal teaching game is *Oregon Settler*, a simulation-based game available on Apple's App Store and Google Play that teaches players about the history of U.S. westward expansion during the 19th century. The game consists of gameplay scenarios where the player is learning valuable information about living in the past. A good testing game is *Grand Prix Multiplication* (http://bit.ly/1ervSCB) hosted by *Arcademic Skill Builders*, a game that only assesses students' previously acquired knowledge and drills them on their multiplication facts.

Differentiating between the two game types is fairly straightforward. If content is introduced to the player, then the game is most likely a teaching game. If it asks questions and expects the answers from the very beginning, then the game fits neatly into the testing category.

Game developers are starting to create more games that are classified as both teaching and testing games. An example of a teaching and testing game is *Teachley: Mt. Multiplis*. In the game, players receive instruction for mathematics computation in a visually appealing learning environment. They also receive constant feedback and reward. The app, available through Apple's App Store, also uses data analytics to measure and track student performance.

Piloting Games

Once teachers have identified a potential game to use with students, we recommend taking time to play them. Reflect on the following questions to determine if the game is ideal for integration into instruction (see figure 4.2, page 62).

Learning Outcomes and Pedagogy

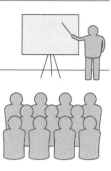

- ☐ Does gameplay support the learning objectives or expected student outcome(s)?

- ☐ Can you use multiple games during instruction to address more or all of the learning objectives or expected student outcome(s)?

- ☐ Is gameplay realistic, and does it involve skills that are useful in the real world?

- ☐ Is the game fun, engaging, and challenging for players?

- ☐ Will the game challenges evolve with better player performance?

- ☐ Is one game better aligned with the expected learning outcomes than the others?

- ☐ Will gameplay address other content areas to provide a multidisciplinary experience for the students?

- ☐ Is the game a teaching game or a testing game? How do you intend to use it with your students?

Assessment

- ☐ Does the game contain assessment tools or performance measurements to provide users and instructors with player feedback?

- ☐ Can the game-based facilitator (educator) incorporate reality-based assessment strategies, measuring knowledge attained during gameplay?

- ☐ How might the game be incorporated into classroom instruction or assessment?

Technical Aspects

- ☐ Is the presentation of the game clearly visible and audible, and does it provide an appealing aesthetic experience?

- ☐ Are there enough game stations to promote a low enough student-to-game ratio?

- ☐ Are appropriate peripherals and accessibility tools provided to each game station for the gaming experience?

- ☐ Is the game control or manipulation transparent, intuitive, and logical for players?

- ☐ Is the digital game content appropriate for the students' academic or maturity level?

Source: Schaaf, 2015, pp. 26–27.

Figure 4.2: Checklist to plan and prepare for a digital game-based learning experience.

*Visit **go.SolutionTree.com/technology** for a reproducible version of this figure.*

This gameplay can't be superficial; you must fully experience the game to critically evaluate it. If the game seems like a good fit with the lesson and the goal (teaching or testing), consider testing the game with a small group of teachers or students. Consult figure 4.2 for the criteria to consider while conducting this piloting process.

Summarizing the Main Points

- The popularity of digital games has given rise to an abundant selection of learning games and apps for educators to use with students.

- Serious games are designed for a purpose other than entertainment. They are designed with a specific objective, such as for social awareness, training purposes, or digital storytelling.

- Finding good learning games is a task that requires research, time, patience, and a bit of luck. It's a process.

- When planning a digital game–based learning experience, educators must consider the game's learning targets, instruction, and assessment.

- Educators should pilot games before implementation so they can fully understand all aspects of the game and foresee any potential issues that might arise with students.

Questions to Consider

1. How do serious games differ from games for entertainment? What benefits do serious games offer learners?

2. As an educator, what platforms are at your disposal to use in your school, institution, or learning center? Are there ways to access additional platforms for student use?

3. What is planning outward? Why is it an easier strategy to use than researching a game that meets specific learning outcomes?

4. What are the criteria educators must consider when selecting and using a digital game for instruction with learners?

5. Why is it important to pilot games and have others review them before use with all students?

Chapter 5

Lesson Design Using Digital Games

Video games foster the mindset that allows creativity to grow.

—Nolan Bushnell

*This chapter is adapted from material in *Using Digital Games as Assessment and Instruction Tools* (Schaaf, 2015), part of Solution Tree Press's *Solutions for Digital Learner–Centered Classrooms* series.

Using digital games and media in meaningful ways within lessons depends far more on the effective use of existing teaching skills than on the development of any new, game-related skills. Digital gaming can be infused into many of the traditional elements of a lesson plan. Educators can use games, YouTube clips, short Vine and Instagram footage, and so much more to provide information to students. Learners can also use these digital media to create authentic instructional artifacts to demonstrate their competencies in written and spoken language and storytelling and their understanding of acquired knowledge.

Short-Form Games

Following are some easy-to-implement instructional strategies educators can use to promote fun and engaging learning experiences using *short-form games* during a lesson. A short-form game takes a short amount of time to complete or master. Each strategy is defined and includes a sample game and a scenario for envisioning the strategy in action.

Lesson Motivation

Many traditional lesson-planning formats include a short motivation or warm-up activity to prime and engage learners for new learning experiences. Educators can easily infuse digital games at this starting point in the lesson. The allotted time should be relatively short—perhaps five to ten minutes. During this time, teachers help students uncover the purpose for gameplay by asking questions to activate prior knowledge and connecting the concepts to the expected learning outcomes for the lesson. Afterward, teachers debrief students to reflect on gameplay and connect it with new concepts or skills being explored in the next learning activity of the lesson.

An example of this strategy is a lesson motivation for a unit on recycling, reusing, and reducing in the environment—a common science and social studies concept in grades 1–5 curriculum. The game *Recycle This!* (http://climatekids.nasa .gov/recycle-this) from Climate Kids: NASA's Eyes on the Earth is a web browser–based game where players make good environmental decisions through recycling or trashing certain household items. Before gameplay, the teacher introduces the game to students, asks them to predict what the game will be about, plays the game for a few moments (while students watch) to introduce game controls and navigation, and then allows them to play. The teacher then asks questions that draw out and examine key concepts explored during gameplay. For *Recycle This!*, questions to ask might include:

- "What were you able to recycle in the game?"
- "Did any items accidently end up in the trash can?"
- "Were there any items you discovered that could be recycled?"
- "What are some things you know you can recycle but weren't in the game?"

Free Play

Free play allows learners to explore digital games with no (or with very little) input from their teachers. This strategy can be used for both short-form and long-form games, but time should be monitored so the free-play period does not extend for too long. Students have free rein to explore, learn, fail, retry, and reflect on the game in an unstructured environment. During free play, the teacher circulates in the learning environment, carefully observing students as they play to learn. The teacher records what he or she witnesses, assists learners who are struggling, and adjusts the learning scenario by changing the skill level, difficulty setting, or selecting a more challenging game if students find it too easy.

An effective follow-up activity should come after free play in which learners demonstrate their mastery of the content, such as through having a classroom discussion, using creative writing, journaling, blogging, creating a multimedia product, or participating in a simulation or role play.

In PBS Kids' *Mad Money* (http://pbskids.org/itsmylife/games/mad_money_flash.html), learners grades 2–4 must save money over the course of thirty days (within the game) to purchase a big-ticket item they select. Players visit shops, perform chores, collect bonuses, and receive penalties on their way to their financial goal. *Mad Money* is user friendly, so players can master how to play it rather quickly. After gameplay, students could demonstrate their learning by researching and creating a monthly budget to either save money or buy an item. This is only one example of how free-play gaming leads to further learning and demonstration of learning.

Baseline to Finish Line

With this strategy, students play the selected game twice—once before formal class instruction on the targeted learning and again after the learning has occurred. This strategy is best used for short-form games, since it requires gamers to play it twice. During the first gaming session, referred to as the *baseline*, the teacher circulates and records student performance (if the game does not already do so) as students play. Students' individual performance becomes a *baseline score*—a raw measure of the student's current understanding of the targeted concepts explored in the game. After instruction, students play the same game again while the teacher observes their performance during a second gameplay session known as the *finish line*. Teachers should see improved performance during gameplay in the second session. Teachers conduct in-progress evaluations to formatively assess student learning needs and academic progress during instruction. They can also consult any game data that are generated by students or ask students to take and share a screenshot of their in-game performance.

An example of this strategy in action comes from Funbrain, which hosts a testing game called the *Periodic Table Game* (www.funbrain.com/funbrain/periodic).

The game asks players to name certain elements when given symbols and tracks correct and incorrect answers. The teacher asks students to play two rounds and records their scores out of a possible twenty points. Students play the baseline round first and then receive a formal lesson involving the periodic table. Then they play the game again—the finish line—with the goal of scoring higher than their baseline scores. Both teachers and students can see academic growth over time. If a student scores lower than, or the same as, his or her baseline score, the student might need reteaching or an alternate approach to learning about the periodic table.

Context

At times, educators can have difficulty demonstrating the importance of what students are learning in class. It is particularly challenging for teachers to demonstrate real-world relevance within the school setting. Digital games help create context. They have the ability to immerse students in new and exciting learning experiences and establish that crucial instructional relevance. First, introduce students to the setting of the game and briefly offer some insights into its significance to the theme or topic of the lesson. Next, have players engage in the gameplay, stopping on occasion to discuss the gameplay and the relevance for playing in the first place. Students can also demonstrate what they have learned by creating an educational artifact (such as a written product, video, or presentation). This strategy can be used for both short-form and long-form games.

A great example of a digital game's ability to create context is *Loot Pursuit: Pompeii* (https://goo.gl/ubMZ61) by Dig-It! Games. The game brings history to life while assessing students' problem-solving skills at their pace. Players must solve challenging and complex mathematics problems involving algebra, geometry, fractions, integers, and ratios to recover more than seventy-five genuine artifacts stolen from the ancient Roman city of Pompeii.

Players must complete the mathematics challenges to progress through the immersive, cross-curricular story line. Game designers have embedded into gameplay mathematics standards involving algebraic thinking, fractions, geometry, and ratios; social studies concepts such as history and civilization; and language arts concepts such as narrative and storytelling. Students can chronicle their experiences playing the game by making a video or keeping a gaming journal.

Anticipation

With this strategy, the teacher selects a game students will play during class. However, before gameplay begins, students get several questions they must answer during or after gameplay to activate their prior knowledge and build curiosity about a new topic or instructional concepts. Teachers can format these questions as multiple choice, true or false, or fill in the blank—any format conducive to quick, short-form responses works well. Teachers allow players to engage in gameplay with little to no interference. After they are finished with the game, students come back together as a class to revisit the anticipation questions.

Mission US: A Cheyenne Odyssey (www.mission-us.org/pages/mission-3) is a role-playing game in which players take on the role of Little Fox, a young Cheyenne boy in the 19th century. As Little Fox, players are immersed in a historical simulation rich in logical reasoning, investigation, and multiculturalism. Before players begin, teachers pose anticipatory guiding questions, such as the following three (Schaaf, 2015).

1. Are the Cheyenne children similar to you? *Yes* or *No*

2. Little Fox belongs to the Northern Cheyenne tribe. *True* or *False*

3. Select the setting the Cheyenne tribe called home. *Mountains*, *Plains*, or *Desert*

Once students have played the game, they revisit their original responses. These short-form questions lead the class into a deeper discussion about the game and its content.

Teams and Tournaments

Digital games are a natural way for students to develop the fundamentals of teamwork and cultivate their collaborative skills. Through team-based games, players begin to understand the basic advantages of cooperative learning, such as the division of labor, the benefit of pooling group knowledge to develop collective intelligence, and increased productivity. Working in collaborative learning groups also develops important interpersonal skills and morals; players explore the concepts of fairness, group dynamics, leadership, and responsibility. Players share a common goal and win or fail as a team. Implementing teams during gameplay also has the benefit of requiring fewer technological resources since players are typically taking turns.

A classic example of a game that can utilize teamwork is *Jeopardy!* JeopardyLabs (https://jeopardylabs.com) allows teachers to create *Jeopardy!* games online for free. JeopardyLabs can provide games for any grade level and academic content area. To play, a teacher divides the class into two teams. Each team takes turns answering review questions while discussing and celebrating or lamenting together.

Tournaments are another team-based game format that uses competition. Typically, teams are smaller for tournament games. In the multiplication game *Grand Prix Multiplication* (http://goo.gl/2qQkMC), the teacher instructs student team members to take turns racing. The goal of the game is to receive the fastest time around a racetrack as players answer multiplication problems. Each team member participates in the race, and all members add their results together for a combined score. The fastest team either wins or moves on to the next stage of the tournament.

When using teams or a tournament structure in an educational gaming environment, teachers must look for ways for students to productively interact, equitably divide work, and share responsibility and accountability for success and failure. Teachers can also design and implement activities outside of the digital game to enhance the collaborative or competitive nature of the gameplay. For example, they can ask students questions, track and reward team progress, or provide players with opportunities to reflect on gameplay or apply their knowledge to a follow-up task, activity, or challenge.

Long-Form Games

The previous section examined ways to use short-form games during instruction. Whether used as a warm-up, a review, a lesson event, or a catalyst for cooperative learning, digital game–based learning fits into many lesson plans, particularly if the game is short enough to complete before moving on to the next part of the lesson. But what about games that do not fit neatly into a ten-minute warm-up, a thirty-minute review, or even a sixty-minute lesson plan? What about long-form games?

Long-form games have extensive story lines or are virtual environments that take players more time to explore than short-form games. The following types of long-form games provide a wealth of opportunities for experiential learning. In addition, they can be a catalyst for students to demonstrate their knowledge through educational artifacts such as creating written products, podcasts, videos, slideshows, mind maps, and journals.

Minecraft and *MinecraftEdu*

Minecraft (https://minecraft.net) is a popular game that has taken the gaming world by storm. Developed by Swedish game developer Mojang, *Minecraft* is an open-world building game where players use blocks to build structures in creative mode. Many educators have taken advantage of the game's popularity and functionality to teach the digital generation.

Playing *Minecraft*, like many long-form games, is an extensive endeavor. For example, the teacher could ask students to replicate a scene from *Romeo and Juliet* within the game. Students would read and re-read the play and do other research for ideas to use in building the setting with blocks within the game. The potential for experiential and multidisciplinary learning more than makes up for the instructional time used during gameplay.

MinecraftEdu (http://minecraftedu.com) realizes the potential of *Minecraft* for learning and offers educational solutions, support, and ideas to integrate the game into schools. Educators use *Minecraft* to explore hundreds of concepts in multiple disciplines. In mathematics classes, players can explore concepts such as addition, subtraction, multiplication, and volume. In history, students can construct historical structures such as the pyramids of Giza or the Roman Colosseum. In science, players can explore concepts such as landforms, the life cycle, and biomes. There are also options for social studies, art, language arts—the list of potential learning experiences educators can facilitate with their students using *Minecraft* goes on and on.

The Sandbox and *The Sandbox EDU*

Pixowl's *The Sandbox* (www.thesandboxgame.com) shares many of the same game characteristics as *Minecraft*. Players craft their universe while exploring resources such as water, soil, lightning, and lava and complex elements such as monuments, wildlife, trees, vehicles, sensors, monuments, and explosives. *The Sandbox* also has an educational version known as *The Sandbox EDU* (www .thesandboxgame.com/education) that includes short-form and long-form lesson ideas and resources for teachers ready to embrace gaming on their Apple devices.

World of Warcraft in School

Educators Peggy Sheehy and Lucas Gillispie developed *World of Warcraft in School* (http://wowinschool.pbworks.com/w/page/5268731/FrontPage)—a language arts curriculum created around the extremely popular and incredibly immersive massively multiplayer online game *World of Warcraft*. The *World of Warcraft in School* website includes a whole unit curriculum and identifies learning targets. The game's narrative-rich story lines provide students with exciting opportunities to develop their reading and writing skills.

Lure of the Labyrinth

Hosted by Thinkport (a product of a partnership between Maryland Public Television and the Johns Hopkins University Center for Technology in Education), *Lure of the Labyrinth* (https://labyrinth.thinkport.org) is a long-form digital game for middle school students learning prealgebra. It includes a wealth of intriguing mathematics-based puzzles embedded in an exciting narrative game in which the ultimate goal is to find a lost pet while saving the world from monsters. The game is linked to the Common Core State Standards and gives students a chance to think like mathematicians.

Although using long-form games requires more time for students to play and learn than short-form games, the investment is time well spent. Students become engaged in numerous learning experiences while immersed in a compelling story line. These games also often have better production quality than the quick-to-produce, short-form games.

Lesson Sparks

Integrating digital games into classroom instruction involves some simple instructional and technical planning. *Lesson sparks* are instructional components that help educators integrate digital games into a technology-enriched curriculum. Lesson sparks are based on content standards and are part of a larger instructional plan or unit. Most digital games are designed without a traditional learning experience in mind, so it may be easier for educators to plan a lesson around existing games. (See planning outward in chapter 4.)

To create a lesson spark, educators start with the content standards they use to develop learning goals. These could include the following.

- Common Core State Standards (www.corestandards.org)
- Mid-continent Research for Education and Learning's (McREL, 2014) Content Knowledge Online Edition (www2.mcrel.org /compendium/browse.asp)
- Individual district or school standards and benchmarks

Since digital games and simulations are forms of interactive technologies, educators must also select technology standards to identify the skills and processes learners will use during their lesson spark experiences. The most influential set of technology standards in the educational technology community are the International Society for Technology in Education (ISTE) Standards for Students (ISTE, 2007; www.iste.org/standards/ISTE-standards/standards-for-students). This set of technology standards identifies the essential skills students need to excel in college and careers and represents what educators should focus on during instruction (see figure 5.1).

1. Creativity and Innovation

2. Communication and Collaboration

3. Research and Information Fluency

4. Critical Thinking, Problem Solving, and Decision Making

5. Digital Citizenship

6. Technology Operations and Concepts

Figure 5.1: ISTE Standards for Students.

When creating lesson sparks involving digital games, teachers use many of the same steps they use during basic lesson planning. They determine the time students will need to complete the spark and all of its components and provide a description of the digital game. It's important to provide the information necessary to establish a basic structure for the lesson spark.

Lessons are made up of numerous events interwoven to create an instructional tapestry. These events can include classroom discussions, hands-on activities, group work, and the construction of some form of educational artifact. Gameplay is one of these lesson events. The lesson event answers the *how* and *what* questions in a teacher's lesson plan, and educators must consider how learners will access the game. This depends on whether students will be engaging in a one-to-one computing environment, working in a classroom with multiple computer stations, or playing on a single computer or gaming station.

The level of instructional integration for digital games differs from game to game. Digital game–based learning experiences can make up a larger instructional unit, such as a whole lesson, unit, or even a course. However, teachers will integrate most instructional gaming experiences into instruction at the event or lesson levels. A digital game that teaches a unit or course is specifically designed to fit the instructional need, so these games are rare.

Following are three lesson spark examples (figures 5.2–5.4, pages 74–78): one for elementary social studies, another for middle school science, and another for high school mathematics and economics. A blank lesson spark template is available for download at **go.SolutionTree.com/technology**.

Gaming Lesson Spark: Around Town	
Grade Level and Subject Area: Grade 1 social studies	**Time Allotted for Lesson Spark:** Twenty minutes

Specific Content Indicator or Objective (from national, state, or district standards):

National Council for the Social Studies (NCSS, 2010)

1. Social studies programs should include experiences that provide for the study of people, places, and environments, so that the learner can:

    b. Interpret, use, and distinguish various representations of the Earth, such as maps, globes, and photographs

    c. Use appropriate resources, data sources, and geographic tools such as atlases, databases, grid systems, charts, graphs, and maps to generate, manipulate, and interpret information

Technology Standards (ISTE, 2007)

1. Creativity and innovation: Students demonstrate creative thinking, construct knowledge, and develop innovative products and processes using technology.

    c. Use models and simulations to explore complex systems and issues.

Integrated Gameplay Level (choose one):

☑ Level 1 (event level)—Game addresses one or numerous events during a lesson.

☐ Level 2 (lesson level)—Game addresses the entire lesson or more than one lesson.

☐ Level 3 (unit or module level)—Game addresses a complete unit or units but not all of the course.

Digital Game
(Give game's name and any links to it or resources describing how the game functions.)
Use Cardinal Directions (www.sfsocialstudies.com/g1/u2/index.html)

Lesson Spark Chronology
(Indicate how and where the gameplay fits into the lesson spark.)
Indicate:

1. How you will introduce students to the instructional digital game

   Students will envision they are traveling around town with their parents to help guide them to the proper destination using cardinal directions.

2. How and when you will disseminate student materials, technology, and resources

   Students will access computer workstations and the game after the teacher has reviewed with them how to interact with the game.

3. What you will ask or tell students about the reason for using the game

   Students will be using cardinal directions to help them locate certain things in the world—specifically a community park, school, and so on.

4. What students will be expected to do

   Students will be expected to navigate the streets using cardinal directions to arrive at the final destination.

5. What students will record, if anything, and in what format and what students should do with what they have recorded or learned

   Students will not need to record anything for this activity. The teacher will circulate to each workstation to witness student performance.

6. What feedback on performance students will receive and how it will be used for future instruction

   The game provides students with verification that they were successful arriving at their final destination. The teacher will reteach or assist any students having difficulty navigating through the game.

Follow-Up
(Briefly describe what the next steps will be after gameplay.)

Students will complete an exit ticket. The exit ticket will be a printed copy of the game screen. Students will pair up with a partner. Partner 1 will pick a start and finish point. Partner 2 will provide directions using cardinal directions to travel to the intended destination.

Figure 5.2: Lesson spark example for grade 1 social studies.

Visit **go.SolutionTree.com/technology** *for a reproducible version of this figure.*

Gaming Lesson Spark: The Relationship of the Earth, Sun, and Moon—It's Only a Phase	
Grade Level and Subject Area: Grade 6 Earth and space science	**Time Allotted for Lesson Spark:** Thirty-five minutes

Specific Content Indicator or Objective (from national, state, or district standards):

Next Generation Science Standards (NGSS Lead States, 2013; middle school space science)

Develop and use a model of the Earth-sun-moon system to describe the cyclic patterns of lunar phases, eclipses of the sun and moon, and seasons.

Technology Standards (ISTE, 2007)

1. Creativity and innovation: Students demonstrate creative thinking, construct knowledge, and develop innovative products and processes using technology.

   c. Use models and simulations to explore complex systems and issues.

Integrated Gameplay Level (choose one):

☑ Level 1 (event level)—Game addresses one or numerous events during a lesson.

☐ Level 2 (lesson level)—Game addresses the entire lesson or more than one lesson.

☐ Level 3 (unit or module level)—Game addresses a complete unit or units but not all of the course.

Digital Game
(Give game's name and any links to it or resources describing how the game functions.)
Phases of the Moon by Wonderville (http://wonderville.org/asset/phases-of-the-moon)

Lesson Spark Chronology
(Indicate how and where the gameplay fits into the lesson spark.)
Indicate:

1. How you will introduce students to the instructional digital game

   While using think-pair-share, students will discuss and share their conceptual understanding of the Earth, sun, and moon and how they move through space. Students can record their beliefs in their science journal and return to the journal at the end of the lesson spark.

2. How and when you will disseminate student materials, technology, and resources

   After completing the think-pair-share, students will access the game online. Students will need headphones to listen to the game's tutorials.

3. What you will ask or tell students about the reason for using the game

   The movement of the Earth, sun, and moon can be difficult to visualize, so we will play the game to help visualize the movement of these celestial objects.

4. What students will be expected to do

   After gameplay, students discuss with their classmates if their original conceptual understanding was correct and how the Earth, sun, and moon move through space and why this movement causes moon phases.

5. What students will record, if anything, and in what format and what students should do with what they have recorded or learned

Students will record key information uncovered during gameplay and sketch a diagram of how the Earth, sun, and moon move through space.

6. What feedback on performance students will receive and how it will be used for future instruction

The game provides checkpoint assessments to check for student understanding. Teachers will use the feedback for reteaching if needed.

Follow-Up
(Briefly describe what the next steps will be after gameplay.)

Students will complete an exit ticket to demonstrate the following.

1. *Describe how the Earth, sun, and moon move through space.*

2. *Explain why humans see phases of the moon from Earth.*

3. *Describe how much of the moon's surface is always lit up by the sun.*

4. *Describe what occurs during a solar eclipse.*

Figure 5.3: Lesson spark example for grade 6 Earth and space science.

Visit go.SolutionTree.com/technology for a reproducible version of this figure.

Gaming Lesson Spark: A Penny Saved	
Grade Level and Subject Area: High school financial literacy	**Time Allotted for Lesson Spark:** Sixty minutes

Specific Content Indicator or Objective (from national, state, or district standards):

Maryland State Curriculum (Maryland State Department of Education, 2016)

Evaluate the financial choices that are made based on available resources, needs, and wants for goods and services.

- Explain how scarcity and opportunity cost affect decision making.
- Analyze costs, benefits, and opportunity cost to determine the achievement of personal financial goals.

Technology Standards (ISTE, 2007)

4. Critical thinking, problem solving, and decision making

    a. Identify and define authentic problems and significant questions for investigation.

    b. Plan and manage activities to develop a solution or complete a project.

Integrated Gameplay Level (choose one):

    ☐ Level 1 (event level)—Game addresses one or numerous events during a lesson.

    ☑ Level 2 (lesson level)—Game addresses the entire lesson or more than one lesson.

    ☐ Level 3 (unit or module level)—Game addresses a complete unit or units, but not all of the course.

continued →

Digital Game
(Give game's name and any links to it or resources describing how the game functions.)

Spent (http://playspent.org/html)

Lesson Spark Chronology
(Indicate how and where the gameplay fits into the lesson spark.)

Indicate:

1. How you will introduce students to the instructional digital game

   Students participate in a short question session. They share how they earn money and what their budgeting practices are. Finally, they theorize how long they can survive on $100 for essentials.

2. How and when you will disseminate student materials, technology, and resources

   Introduce learners to Spent. *In the game, players must manage their income and expenses for the month to avoid going bankrupt.*

3. What will you ask or tell students about the reason for using the game

   Inform students that the game will progress through a month. During this time, players are responsible for making good financial decisions and not losing all of their money. Ask students to select one of the challenging scenarios that comes up during gameplay and record it to use after gameplay.

4. What students will be expected to do

   Ask students to share their game performance with the class. Ask the class to reflect on students' performance and judge how they progressed through the month.

5. What students will record, if anything, and in what format and what students should do with what they have recorded or learned

   Students will not record information during gameplay.

6. What feedback on performance students will receive and how it will be used for future instruction

   Each student must recall one of the situations he or she experienced during gameplay. Do students feel they made the right decision in a particular instance? Why or why not? Teachers will use the student decisions in a follow-up conversation and analysis.

Follow-Up
(Briefly describe what the next step will be after gameplay.)

Each student is responsible for creating a one-month budget that includes a theoretical job, rent, food, and other expenses.

Figure 5.4: Lesson spark example for high school financial literacy.

*Visit **go.SolutionTree.com/technology** for a reproducible version of this figure.*

Summarizing the Main Points

- Short-form games are games that take a short period of time to complete. Long-form games take a longer period of time to complete.

- There are many strategies to consider when implementing digital games in instruction. There is free play, using gameplay as a lesson motivation or anticipation task, using games in a baseline to finish-line format, or in a team or tournament competition, to name a few.

- There are many short-form and long-form games available for educators to use to create immersive learning experiences for students.

- *Lesson sparks* are instructional plans that allow educators to prepare digital game–based learning experiences for their learners.

Questions to Consider

1. What game type would you prefer to use during instruction— short form or long form? What unique challenges would each type of game present to educators and students?

2. After reading this chapter (and previous chapters), do you have an idea for a game to incorporate into instruction? If so, what strategy will you use with learners?

3. What lesson sparks will you create? Will you share them with colleagues or other teachers?

Chapter 6
Digital Gaming and Assessment

Assessment (specifically summative assessment) has long been considered an unpleasant task for students, and it has gained a similar reputation as unpleasant among teachers as well (Nichols, & Berliner, 2005). High-stakes testing has created an atmosphere of tension, competition, and stress. For many educators, high-stakes testing and assessments have become the driving force for everything they do. High-stakes testing determines what students will learn, where they will learn it, what academic programs will be funded, what equipment teachers will use, how teacher performance will be evaluated, and even if teachers and schools receive penalties. This testing approach stifles educators and students alike. In fact, many schools sacrifice curriculum and rigor to prepare students to test well.

By definition, *summative assessments* evaluate student learning at the end of an instructional unit or period by comparing student scores against some standard or benchmark. Summative assessments can be useful—for example, in determining strengths and weaknesses in curriculum design and instructional delivery. They can also provide a very detailed snapshot of the learner if the assessment is well-aligned to instruction; however, this type of assessment only provides a one-dimensional glimpse. Educators, administrators, parents, and policymakers should be careful to not settle for a single snapshot to determine a student's academic success. Educators and stakeholders should seek to see the entire photo album. Thus, summative assessment results should be only one performance data point of many. Summative assessment data has its place in education but not as the driving force for implementing education reform, acquiring and allocating school funding, and determining teachers' effectiveness. If testing data determines that a school system is not serving its students in the classroom, then actions must be taken to correct the situation. However, when testing becomes the ultimate indicator of success and failure for a student, school, or district, it takes what matters most—our students—and quantifies them as a simple data point.

Imagine a young learner; let's call her Eve. She is a bright, articulate student who is energetic, sociable, creative, and hardworking. She takes a timed test filled with low-order thinking questions asking her to recall what she has memorized or read in a dense block of text. She fails miserably. Eve is not dumb. She is not lazy. She doesn't struggle with a learning disability or a developmental issue. She is not a slow learner. She may have failed because she has test anxiety or was sick the days leading up to the test, or she may not have understood the importance of the test.

Eve is a student learning in an education system that depends too heavily on summative assessments to weigh student, school, district, and national success. Assessment must be a process in which teachers and students come together to determine where students are now, where they want to go in the future, and what path they will take to get from here to there. Assessment does not have to anesthetize Eve. It should invigorate her and others to set a course for academic success. That's where digital games come in.

Digital Games and Summative Assessment

What if students took standardized tests by playing a digital game? Digital games' mechanics and narratives can be designed to measure not only content-specific knowledge but also soft skills such as problem solving, creativity, and collaboration. Many education research institutions and think tanks are already working on creating powerful learning and assessment experiences for the digital generation. For example, GlassLab explores "the potential for existing, commercially successful digital games to serve both as potent learning environments and real-time assessments of student learning" (Institute of Play, 2014). However, we do not recommend that educators use digital games found in a catalog or through a web search for the purpose of summative assessment. Teachers must align instruction and assessment, or it could spell disaster for the learner.

For example, if a student plays digital mathematics games for instructional purposes and then takes a pencil-and-paper quiz based on the concepts explored during gameplay, he or she is participating in a misaligned assessment. How does the teacher know the student will be able to transfer his or her game-based learning experiences to the traditional quiz? The teacher is changing too many variables for the assessment results to be valid and reliable. It would serve everyone best if the teacher would use traditional instruction along with traditional assessment types like tests and quizzes. At least the instruction would be aligned with the assessment type. Teachers must align instruction to assessment methods (Martone & Sireci, 2009).

However, there is a place for digital games in summative assessment; teachers don't have to wait for game designers to get the learning-and-assessment formula just right. Digital games are valuable tools to use to review and prepare for summative assessments. Cognitive scientists find great promise in *spaced repetition*—the process of learners studying information in blocks over longer periods of time. Instead of cramming study sessions into a short time frame, the learner learns and relearns content over an extended period. "The spacing effect is one of the oldest and best-documented phenomena in the history of learning and memory research" (Bahrick & Hall, 2005, as cited in Thalheimer, 2006, p. 3). When digital game review sessions over an extended time frame use spaced repetition, content sticks for learners with both unit and standardized tests (Bahrick & Hall, 2005, as cited in Thalheimer, 2006). The added benefits include engagement, fun, and excitement.

Educators can create these review games using numerous tools. Whatever the tool, it should be easy to use, versatile, and adaptable to numerous classroom environments. Socrative (www.socrative.com) lets teachers engage and assess their students with instructional activities on most digital devices. Ryan, an assistant professor of technology, conducts a review session for his final exam using Socrative with his graduate-level students. The students are split into two teams and play a quiz game to prepare for the final exam. The students get to practice answering questions for the test in an instructional format that not only allows them to get answers wrong but also learn from their mistakes. Many of Ryan's students credit the review game for helping them prepare for the final exam in his course.

Through the use of real-time questioning, instant result aggregation, and visualization, teachers can determine students' understanding. QuizBreak!

(http://clear.msu.edu/quizbreak), Plickers (https://plickers.com), and Review Game Zone (http://reviewgamezone.com) are free tools educators can use to construct their own review games.

Digital Games and Formative Assessment

Unlike summative assessment, which occurs at the end of the instructional process, *formative assessment* is ongoing. Both teachers and students use it to evaluate and make adjustments during the learning experience. It's a critical way for teachers to check students' understanding and then use the information to guide instruction.

Formative assessment helps create and renew the learning process. Unlike the linear design of summative assessment, formative assessment is more like a cycle. Educators continuously guide students to access their prior knowledge, engage them in learning activities to build on their knowledge base, help them to demonstrate their instructional gains (through a variety of assessment methods), and then reflect with them on the learning. After completing this cycle, the entire process begins anew.

Educators who use digital games to formatively assess facts and knowledge, concepts, big ideas, and mastery of specific skills are more likely to track student progress, give feedback to students, and check for student engagement and motivation on a daily basis (Fishman, Riconscente, Snider, Tsai, & Plass, 2014). Teachers who use digital games during instruction are also more likely to use formative assessment techniques in their classrooms by observing students, having classroom discussions, reviewing student work, using every-pupil response, asking probing and guiding questions, and peeking over students' shoulders during work time (Fishman et al., 2014). "Teachers . . . are more likely to use information from formative assessment to track student progress and give students feedback on a daily basis" (Fishman et al., 2014, p. 24) This feedback is vital for individual student growth and academic goal setting.

BrainPOP has a feature in its GameUp digital-game collection (www.brainpop .com/games) that is a wonderful example of using formative assessment during gameplay. The SnapThought tool allows students to take a screenshot of their gameplay and publish a reflective journal entry they can then send to their teacher. The journal entry allows students to demonstrate their mastery of a new skill, provide evidence of new content knowledge, produce an assessment artifact for evaluation, and help teachers make informed instructional decisions related to their students' future learning experiences.

Stealth Assessment

According to Valerie Shute and Matthew Ventura (2013), *stealth assessment* is assessment that is woven directly and invisibly into the fabric of the learning or gaming environment. During gameplay, students naturally produce rich sequences of actions while performing complex tasks, drawing on the same skills or competencies that educators want to assess.

Instead of isolating the assessment from the learning process, it is embedded in it; students are constantly learning and being evaluated. Stealth assessment also prevents students from being affected by test anxiety, thus test data will be a more accurate representation of student knowledge. Since stealth assessment is situational (embedded in gameplay), the learner is "focused on the situation, which provides a better approximation of how he or she would behave in a similar real-world situation" (Derosier, 2014).

For educators, using stealth assessment might seem like a far-fetched dream. However, digital games can capture just as much data as they transmit to the player. Educators can also use traditional means of assessment, such as classroom observation, to assess student performance and make informed instructional decisions. As learning games continue to evolve, their assessment capacities will become more robust and transparent for educators to use with their students for deep, powerful learning.

Learning Analytics

Educators champion their students' academic growth every day. However, no matter how well trained and observant teachers are, they can't capture every single achievement, success, obstacle, mistake, or challenge that each of their fifteen, twenty, thirty, or even one hundred students experience every day. After all, teachers are only human (albeit incredibly hardworking and dedicated humans).

Technology systems like computers, tablets, gaming consoles, and mobile devices can easily collect user data. The user's every choice, answer, and experience can be logged and stored automatically. This unbelievable access to raw data has created a powerful mathematical science known as *data analytics*. Many companies and organizations use data analytics to make better business decisions. The sciences use digital analytics to verify or disprove theories. Education's variant of this science is known as *learning analytics*. Instead of technology systems logging consumer behavior and purchase habits, which are commonly the case with data analytics, learning analytics focuses on student data like online behavior, assessment results, and learning preferences. Digital games serve as a platform for learning analytics (Gee & Shaffer, 2010). They can provide statistically supported evidence of what works and doesn't in the classroom. If designed appropriately, digital games can capture so many data points about players that they become like a second set of eyes for the teacher.

For example, games can collect the number of correct and incorrect answers a player provides, how the player progresses through a story line or narrative, and even capture exact moments in gameplay while at the same time providing immediate feedback and reward to the player. Educators can use these data to improve their instruction and target students who need extra assistance.

Teachley's (www.teachley.com) games and apps provide the perfect example of learning analytics at work in digital games. Teachley is an educational technology company whose mission is to improve and help shape the future of teaching and learning. Founded by former teachers and experts in children's cognition and learning, Teachley uses cognitive science research to create educational apps that teach effective learning strategies and assess what kids know within engaging games (Carpenter, Pager, & Labrecque, 2013). *Addimal Adventure* and *Mt. Multiplis* are two teaching games that introduce players to memorization and problem-solving strategies to learn operational fluency in early mathematics education. These two games, available on Apple's App Store, are impressive enough, but the background data collection and analytics are truly revolutionary. Figure 6.1 is a screenshot of *Addimal Adventure*, which shows a question example and the strategies the game teaches players.

Teachley analytics collects students' user data as they play and generates reports for educators to analyze. These reports help educators immediately determine students who are excelling in their computational practices, as well as those who need additional support. The games also provide learners with considerable feedback to assist them in setting future learning goals. Figure 6.2 (p. 88) shows a sample report sent to a teacher showing each student and score, the benchmarks, playing time, and intervention.

Source: Courtesy of Teachley © 2016.

Figure 6.1: *Addimal Adventure* gameplay.

Teachley is not the only game developer bringing web-tracking practices into the classroom. *VocabularySpellingCity* (www.spellingcity.com) provides spelling, vocabulary, writing, and language arts activities for K–12 cross-curricular word study. Educators using *VocabularySpellingCity* can automate the administration and grading of spelling and vocabulary tests. It also provides educators with progress monitoring and the option to differentiate learning experiences for students when necessary. For science education, *Science4Us* (www.science4us.com) provides young students with interactive simulations and games from which students can learn.

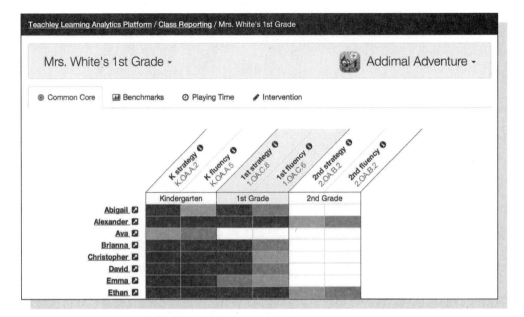

Source: Courtesy of Teachley © 2016.

Figure 6.2: Example *Addimal Adventure* learning analytics progress report.

All of these digital learning game sites offer just-in-time training, support, and lesson ideas so educators do not have to reinvent the wheel when it comes to planning learning experiences for their students. Educators have a choice of using the extensive resources provided by Teachley or simply have students play the game to learn the content and mathematics strategies.

Digital games have great potential for use during both summative and formative assessment. In essence, games are assessments. They test players with every single in-game decision players must make. They are also able to provide immediate feedback based on player decisions. Digital games capture game data, which is useful for educators in terms of assessment. The role of learning analytics could be a game changer in how data is collected in local schools, states, or provincial systems—and perhaps one day, global systems—to help educators improve the ways they teach their students.

Summarizing the Main Points

- A *summative assessment* is given at predetermined intervals and focuses on outcomes. Some examples include national and state assessments, benchmark tests, and final tests or quizzes. Summative assessments specifically test the knowledge that a student should have mastered by a particular point in time. They are often used for student and teacher accountability.

- *Formative assessment* is used to gain an understanding of what students know (and don't know) in order to make responsive changes in teaching and learning approaches. Unlike the linear design of summative assessment, formative assessment is more like a cycle. Educators continuously guide students to access their prior knowledge, engage them in learning activities to build on their knowledge base, help them to demonstrate their instructional gains, and then reflect and provide meaningful feedback on their performances. After completing this cycle, the entire process begins anew.

- *Stealth assessment* is assessment that is unobtrusive to the learning process. It is woven into the learning cycle. Digital games perform stealth assessment because players are unaware their performance is being assessed.

- Digital game–based learning can provide both summative and formative assessment experiences for learners.

- Technology systems can easily capture player performance data. This use of learning analytics can help educators understand their students' abilities and academic needs.

Questions to Consider

1. How can you use digital games in your classroom to enhance or provide both formative and summative assessments?

2. As an educator, what assessment strategies might you use in your classroom?

3. What is stealth assessment? What potential does it offer educators and students alike?

4. What potential does learning analytics offer both learners and educators? Why are digital games an ideal vehicle for using learning analytics?

Chapter 7

The Nine I's of Modern Learning

The curriculum tells you WHAT to teach, but it doesn't tell you HOW.
The how is up to YOU.

—Nicky Mohan

Many countries in the connected world have implemented a standards-based curriculum in their schools. These standards represent a common final destination in the learning process, but the methods and approaches educators and learners use to get to the destination can differ. Many educators, politicians, and parents don't realize that standards are not a prescription on how to teach.

If a standards-based curriculum is a countrywide road trip, then the standards represent checkpoints throughout the journey. Educators and learners are the drivers during this trip, and their learning paths will differ. Perhaps some educators and learners take the most direct route while others take a scenic tour, and in some cases they may get lost on the way or arrive at an unplanned destination. The routes (curriculum) and driving practices (strategies, philosophies, and methodologies) individual educators use should lead to the same destination in the end.

Regardless of the route taken and the driving practices used, teaching with success in the age of academic standards requires engaging and immersive pedagogies.

In the 21st century, it's not about making students learn—it's about getting them to want to learn.

Schools are often so focused on preparing students for short-term goals—the next topic, standard, or test—that there is no time to prepare students for life after school. How can we address short-term goals of preparing students for exams as well as simultaneously addressing long-term goals of preparing them for life? How do we meet the need for students to learn both the traditional curriculum content and the essentials of modern learning?

Using a fun, immersive, and engaging medium such as digital gaming together with gameful design has great potential to engage students and invigorate lessons while simultaneously addressing the mandates of content standards.

The first thing we need to understand is that the traditional emphasis on literacy, while absolutely important, is no longer enough. We need to move our teaching goals beyond the focus on just 20th century literacies to equipping students with the essentials of modern learning. These essentials are mental processes students can learn, develop, practice, and apply as unconscious habits of mind.

These new mental processes are essential skills that pave the way to success in the modern world. There are two major steps in displaying these skills. First, there is the conscious application of them—in other words, students use them, but they have to think about how to use them. This is a very necessary and useful stage in skill development. Think back to when you were learning to drive. At first you were very conscious about turning the steering wheel, stepping on the brakes, stepping on the gas, using the turn signals, checking the mirrors, and so on. Learning all of these things was a necessary step, which is why we don't just give student drivers their licenses. They are just not ready to drive independently without an experienced driver being there to help them learn the necessary skills; they have to constantly think about applying these new skills. Student drivers don't drive the car smoothly. They lurch, stall, and stop abruptly. In the beginning, driving is a halting, uneven, and uncomfortable experience. To become independent drivers, students need sufficient practice and experience so they can learn to apply all of these skills unconsciously and intuitively. Experienced drivers can perform all of these driving skills at a high level. They drive smoothly and are still be able to carry on conversations with their passengers, sip water, and listen to music. That's because they don't have to think; they just drive.

The second major step is having reached a level of unconscious skill. When a driver reaches an unconscious skill level, he or she is able to move to higher-level cognitive functions and not just respond to but also anticipate what other drivers are going to do and take corrective or preventative actions before something happens. This unconscious skill level doesn't just apply to driving; it also applies to reading, writing, arithmetic, research, and problem solving.

So what are the essential skills for modern learning? What are the critical skills that all students need to know at an unconscious level above and beyond an understanding of the traditional content areas? Ted McCain (as referenced in Jukes et al., 2015) has found that people consistently identify nine essential skills that they believe must become an increasing focus of teaching and learning to keep schools relevant in the modern changing world.

In fact, we believe these skills are as important as reading and writing were for success in the 20th century. These are not optional skills. We call these essential skills the *nine I's of modern learning.* (See figure 7.1.)

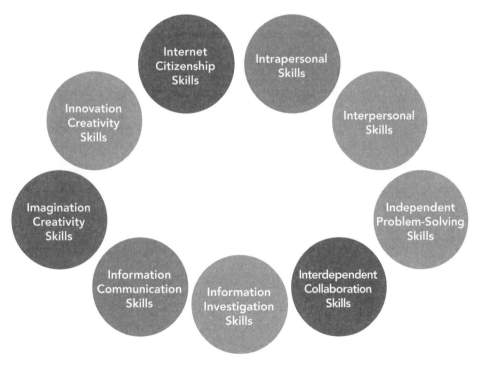

Source: McCain, 2015. Courtesy of Infosavvy21.

Figure 7.1: The nine I's of modern learning.

Intrapersonal Skills

Intrapersonal skills are internal skills, attitudes, emotions, feelings, perceptions, dispositions, and attitudes that occur within a person's mind. Art L. Costa and Bena Kallick (2000) call these the *habits of mind*—skills individuals use to work through real-world situations that allow them to respond using awareness, thought, and intentional strategy to gain a positive outcome. Self-esteem, emotional intelligence, open-mindedness, emotional management, self-confidence, patience and persistence, awareness, straightforwardness, self-worth, and self-realization—these intrapersonal skills are the absolute foundation of everyday life, but aren't typically introduced to students in any structured manner.

Games, both digital and nondigital, help players cultivate their metacognitive skills because they require players to manage their emotions, exercise patience and persistence, encourage reflection and self-criticism, build character through useful failure, and promote growth in emotional intelligence. In the process of playing the games, players learn a great deal about themselves and how they think (and how they *think* they think—metacognition) through the trials, tribulations, and triumphs of gameplay.

Interpersonal Skills

The second I is for interpersonal skills. One of the vital differences between intrapersonal and interpersonal communication is that *intrapersonal* intelligence has to do with behavior that is within a person while *interpersonal* abilities have to do with understanding and comprehending other people and situations. Interpersonal skills are the life skills we use every day to communicate and interact with other people, both individually and collectively. These skills also include verbal and nonverbal communication, the ability to listen and ask questions, manners, problem solving, social and cultural awareness, self-management, personal responsibility and accountability, and assertiveness. Having a well-balanced repertoire of interpersonal skills allows individuals to handle complex situations with grace.

Games provide players with opportunities to both compete and collaborate. Many games provide players the chance to ask questions when they are confused, encourage experienced players to assist novices, and in the case of team-based gaming, put aside personal interests for the benefit of a team—practices that are highly valued in today's modern workplace. Although games may seem to be an unlikely place to learn people skills, they provide the opportunity for players to hone them in an environment that is less critical than a boardroom sales pitch.

Independent Problem-Solving Skills

The third I is for independent problem solving, which involves students learning a structured mental process they can use to solve complex problems in real time. There has been a significant shift in the skills needed to function in the modern workplace. The shift is away from physical work and low-level thinking skills toward creative higher-level thinking skills. Computers already perform many low-level thinking tasks. Projecting this trend out to the future suggests that the demand for high-level thinking skills will only expand as we move forward into a world where humans increasingly work alongside smart systems and autonomous robots (Tercek, 2015). Learning a structured mental process for solving problems helps students become analytical thinkers who can compare, contrast, evaluate, synthesize, and apply their new knowledge to answer difficult questions and solve problems in real time independently, without instruction or supervision. In other words, students need the ability to use the higher-order thinking skills in Bloom's taxonomy (1956)—skills that can be explained, learned, practiced, applied, and internalized into unconscious habits of mind.

Many games require players to solve complex real-world problems in real time using a range of evolving strategies. These games provide forgiving environments that encourage players to experiment with different strategies, encourage them to try again when they fail, and progressively reward them for risk taking, persistence, ingenuity, and eventually success. This is the basis of independent problem solving.

Digital games contain powerful systems that simultaneously support and challenge players. Good games tend to start easy and allow the player to develop his or her understanding of the game and its rules. As the player improves, the difficulty level increases, so the player continues to be challenged. Gaming systems are a type of advanced computer intelligence that mimic many of the smart agents or artificial intelligence young players will interact with as they get older and enter the modern workforce.

Good games provide players with the opportunity to repeatedly practice a structured mental process that our colleague and friend Ted McCain (2015) developed to solve problems. He calls this process the *six Ds of problem solving*: (1) defining the problem, (2) discovering how others have addressed it in the past, (3) dreaming of possible solutions, (4) designing a detailed plan for solving it, (5) delivering what you've planned, and (6) debriefing both the results accomplished and the process undertaken in order to improve performance.

Gamers unconsciously and repeatedly apply the six Ds during gameplay. The perfect example of this process in action is during the iCivics games. In the game *Argument War,* the challenge is to argue a constitutional issue in front of the Supreme Court of the United States. The introduction of the game defines the challenge for players. Through gameplay, players must perform both in-game and out-of-game research to discover more information about the topic and to understand how people have approached constitutional problems in the past. Players must then conceptualize and execute a strategic plan to win the game; in this particular game, they must win the argument. Finally, players carry out the game plan and reflect on their victory or defeat. Therefore, throughout gameplay of *Argument Wars,* students have progressed through the six Ds with the mental process of solving problems in modern learning.

Interdependent Collaboration Skills

The next of the nine I's is interdependent collaboration. Being able to work with others on a project has always been an important skill. But today, with the development of global online communications and shared productivity tools like Skype and Google Docs, being able to collaborate both physically and virtually has become an essential skill for all. Interdependent collaboration can be in person or virtual, and it can be synchronous or asynchronous. *Synchronous* means it happens in real time, where collaborative partners simultaneously work and communicate together. Or, it can be *asynchronous*, where collaborative partners work and communicate using collaborative software, but they're not working in the same place or communicating at the same time. In the new digital landscape, interdependent collaboration is a critical skill.

Advancements in gaming technologies allow players to communicate, collaborate, and compete in large gaming communities. These online environments are immensely powerful and allow players to pool their knowledge to improve and evolve in their gameplay. Online communities generate thousands of hours of YouTube how-to videos, game walkthroughs, strategy guides, and discussion forums. A game example that demonstrates this participatory culture is *World of Warcraft*. Many players spend hours strategizing and playing with their team (in the game, their *clan* or *tribe*). Each clan must perform missions known as quests to succeed and become more experienced. In fact, educators Peggy Sheehy and Lucas Gillispie have created an entire language arts curriculum known as *World of Warcraft in School*. (See page 72 for more information on this game.) The participatory elements of gaming communities promote strategic planning, shared productivity, and often have the potential to cultivate digital citizenship. If learning networks could inherit the traits of gaming communities, they would truly be powerful environments for modern-day learning where players worked together to learn and grow.

Information Investigation Skills

The next I is information investigation. In an age of hyper-information, we don't want students who simply consume and regurgitate theoretical knowledge without questioning and validating what they have read or seen. Rather, we need students who are critical and are consistently able to differentiate between the good, bad, and ugly of information sources as they investigate and solve real-world problems.

Information is a valuable commodity in gameplay because digital games invariably contain a great deal of rapidly presented, ever-changing information. It is essential that players be able to sort quickly through multiple streams of cascading information sources to determine what information is vital and what is merely a distraction. Games promote rapid mental processing for the simple reason that if the player is too slow in responding to the information, he or she may get stuck or lose. C. Shawn Green and Daphne Bavelier (2003) reinforce this observation in their study in *Nature*, which determines that action-packed video games measurably improve visual processing skills. An example of this is *Ether One Redux*, available on GOG (www.gog.com/game/ether_one). In this game, players must investigate and solve puzzles to advance in the story line. Secondary and higher education instructors can use this game to examine story lines, characters, and complex time lines.

Information Communication Skills

The next critical skill is information communication. In an increasingly visual world, graphic design must be an everyday part of the curriculum at every grade level and in every subject area for every student. Students must be able to analyze, interpret, and communicate information as effectively in multimedia formats as the older generations were taught to analyze, interpret, and communicate with text and speech. Information communication skills are absolutely foundational for the modern world. Every student and every teacher needs to know modern reading techniques, the principles of graphic design and typography, the principles of color use, the principles of photo and video composition, and how to use visual information to effectively communicate with others.

Many video games are literally and figuratively works of art—masterpieces of programming, art, design, music, and functionality. The more captivating the gaming environment and interface are, the better chance players will immerse themselves in these new virtual worlds. Today's high-quality video games also encourage modern learners to explore design because they want to be creative and design their own games one day. In fact, game-design programs such as Gamestar Mechanic (https://gamestarmechanic.com), GameMaker (www.yoyogames.com/gamemaker), and Scratch (https://scratch.mit.edu) are extremely popular with learners who want to tinker and program their own games.

Imagination Creativity Skills

The next I is imagination creativity. It has two aspects. First, imagination creativity skills can imagine new ways to communicates ideas, messages, and stories more powerfully. These are the new ideas needed for a short story, poem, novel, script, or screenplay that communicate thoughts creatively. The second aspect of imagination creativity is using your imagination to come up with new designs to convey meaning and add value beyond its normal function across multiple forms of media. A nondigital example of this would be adding a nail pull on the other end of a hammer. You have merged two tools into one.

Popular games are powerful forms of media that astonish players with their graphics and premise. Most of the dynamic games such as *Minecraft*, *The Sandbox*, and *SimCity* allow players to create and share their work with others. These games allow players to create, destroy, and recreate again almost instantly. If a player thinks it, he or she can create it, and that is at the core of imagination creativity.

Innovation Creativity Skills

The next I is innovation creativity. In a world of incredible diversity, educators must present learners with problems that have more than one possible solution.

Students are much more likely to encounter open-ended tasks in their personal and professional lives than they are to experience challenges for which there is only one answer (which is often the norm in schools and a complete disconnect with what students experience in the real world).

Many games have challenging problems with numerous ways of solving them. For example, in the classic *Super Mario Bros.*, Mario or Luigi can defeat the evil Bowser using two methods. The first method is using fireballs to zap Bowser and rescue the princess. The second method calls for Mario or Luigi to run underneath Bowser as he jumps to get to the other side of the bridge. Once they are off the bridge, Mario or Luigi uses an ax to chop down the bridge and let Bowser fall into the lake of fire. Both of these methods have the same result and win the game for the player.

Many problems in the real world have multiple solutions. Games help prepare players for the possibility of solving problems in the real world using different solutions, such as prior knowledge, trial and error, or educated guesses.

Internet Citizenship Skills

The final I is Internet citizenship. Before you provide your teenager with the keys to the car, it is essential that you establish clear and concise expectations, train him or her, and provide the appropriate guidance so he or she learns to drive safely. In the same manner, before students are let loose upon the digital landscape and modern world, they must receive guidance related to appropriate ethical practices. However, many educators and parents alike hand over digital devices freely, without a second thought. Developing Internet citizenship skills is like offering an extensive driver's education program so the digital generation will know how to "drive" on the information superhighway.

As previously discussed, many games require collaboration. Jane McGonigal (2011a), epic game designer and author of the best-selling book *Reality Is Broken: Why Games Make Us Better and How They Can Change the World*, identifies the essence of social fabric as gamers working together or competing against many to create a better world. Both digital and nondigital games promote collaboration and competition as a shared goal. YouTube is saturated with how-to videos, fan fiction, and digital mash-ups. Some content developers have millions of followers or views via social media. Video games have captured the focus of the digital generation and created an expansive population of gamers.

Ryan plays a game called *Clash of Clans*. He belongs to a clan that consists of thirty other players; some of these players are located within the continental United States, some live in South Korea, a few live in Australia, and there is even a player from the Philippines. The clan, known as *Fishers of Men*, works together to donate troops, develop and train new clan members, and win wars against other clans. Win or lose, the clan, which is composed of people from different cultures, plays the game together to accomplish shared goals.

Nonetheless, with a new digital landscape and an ever-growing gaming culture come new responsibilities and roles. These new edicts include the need to treat others fairly, with respect and dignity; to accept a person's differences as well as his or her similarities; and to treat others as you would like to be treated. Internet citizenship is now the new Golden Rule.

Present-Day Instruction With the Future in Mind

The nine I's help educators prepare their students for the needs of the present. Students need to master the standards and perform well on mandated tests to be prepared for higher education and their future careers; however, educators must also engage students using exciting and immersive teaching approaches to fulfill over 15,000 hours of instructional time in a K–12 learning career. Learning through the use of games is exciting for students, many of whom have been using gaming for the purpose of learning since before they began their formal education.

Focusing on the nine I's goes beyond preparing students for their present needs. It prepares students for the future—a future that requires them to be excellent problem solvers, communicators, and lifelong learners; a future in which they must be adaptable and resilient to survive and thrive in a volatile, competitive, and ever-evolving globalized job market; a future where humans will cure cancer, end hunger, and travel the stars.

Summarizing the Main Points

- The nine I's of modern learning are essential skills for the 21st century.

- Intrapersonal skills are internal skills, attitudes, emotions, feelings, perceptions, dispositions, and attitudes.

- Interpersonal skills are the life skills we use every day to communicate and interact with other people, both individually and collectively.

- Independent problem-solving skills involve students learning a structured mental process they can use to solve complex problems in real time.

- Interdependent collaboration skills represent collaboration that can occur in person or virtually, and it can be synchronous or asynchronous.

- Information investigation skills represent the practice of validating and authenticating materials students use in their research.

- Information communication skills represent the ability for learners to analyze, interpret, and communicate information in multimedia formats.

- Imagination creativity skills have learners imagine new ways to communicate ideas, messages, and stories. They also require learners to come up with new designs to convey meaning and add value across many media.

- Innovation creativity skills require educators to provide learners with problems with multiple solutions so they can solve problems in unique ways.

- Internet citizenship skills require students to conduct themselves civilly and ethically online.

Questions to Consider

1. Along with learning targets derived from standards, what are the other skills educators must cultivate within their students for modern learning?

2. In your opinion, why are the nine I's such crucial skills for modern learning?

3. How do digital game–based learning and gamification fit into the nine I's of modern learning?

Chapter 8

Universal Design for Learning With Games

It is not the beauty of a building you should look at; it's the construction of the foundation that will stand the test of time.

—David Allan Coe

From the pyramids of Egypt to the Burj Khalifa in Dubai, designing and constructing structures to serve their occupants is a painstaking task. Architects must conceptualize a structure that meets the needs of its occupants before the first hole is dug, the first brick is laid, and the first pipe is welded. Perhaps one of the biggest challenges architects and designers face is that the population they are serving is not one-size-fits-all. How will people in wheelchairs use stairs? How will people with vision loss find room numbers? How will a deaf individual know that a fire alarm is going off?

Architects and designers must think universally and develop solutions to meet the needs of everyone. Buildings have elevators, extra-wide bathroom stalls, Braille room numbers, and fire alarms with both visual and auditory cues. Whether they are called *modifications*, *adaptations*, *interventions*, or *innovations*, these design elements attempt to improve efficiency, safety, aesthetics, and the quality of life for all people. And these modifications aren't just designed for people with disabilities or challenges. Universal design is about providing access to everyone.

Universal Design for Learning

Now, what if educators assumed this same mentality for their students and created materials that would help all learners understand lesson content? What if educators delivered lessons using an engaging, multifaceted approach? What if they helped students create short- and long-term goals for their academic success and rewarded them when their goals were met? Finally, what if educators, much in the same way as architects, could "provide it all" for their diverse students?

Designing and delivering instruction to diverse learners can evolve with the same universal design philosophy architects employ. Learners have unique academic strengths, learning preferences, cultural backgrounds, and life experiences that must be factored into teaching, learning, and the assessment of that learning. This philosophy of designing and delivering a more personalized form of instruction for a diverse student population sounds appealing, but how does a teacher do it short of creating an individual lesson plan for each student, each day?

The Center for Applied Special Technology (CAST, 2011) has developed and refined a framework of principles "for curriculum development that gives all individuals equal opportunities to learn." These principles, known as the Universal Design for Learning (UDL) guidelines (see figure 8.1), "provide a blueprint for creating instructional goals, methods, materials, and assessments that work for everyone—not a single, one-size-fits-all solution but rather flexible approaches that can be customized and adjusted for individual needs" (CAST, 2011).

The UDL guidelines are not meant to be a prescription, but rather they are a set of strategies that can be employed to overcome the barriers inherent in most existing curricula. They may serve as the basis for building in the options and the flexibility that are necessary to maximize learning opportunities for all students (CAST, 2011).

Adopting these guidelines does not require new training or extensive research. They require the same best practices educators are currently employing during their instruction. The true efficacy in these guidelines is how their very philosophy encourages educators and students alike to use multiple approaches and strategies to reach all learners. Educators, curriculum experts, or learning facilitators ingrain multiple UDL indicators as they prepare student and teacher materials, identify instructional and assessment strategies, and implement motivational techniques to deliver multidimensional lessons to a set of diverse learners.

Universal Design for Learning Guidelines		
I. Providing multiple means of representation leads to resourceful, knowledgeable learners.	II. Providing multiple means of action and expression leads to strategic, goal-directed learners.	III. Providing multiple means of engagement leads to purposeful, motivated learners.
1: Provide options for perception 1.1 Offer ways of customizing the display of information 1.2 Offer alternatives for auditory information 1.3 Offer alternatives for visual information	4: Provide options for physical action 4.1 Vary the methods for response and navigation 4.2 Optimize access to tools and assistive technologies	7: Provide options for recruiting interest 7.1 Optimize individual choice and autonomy 7.2 Optimize relevance, value, and authenticity 7.3 Minimize threats and distractions
2: Provide options for language, mathematical expressions, and symbols 2.1 Clarify vocabulary and symbols 2.2 Clarify syntax and structure 2.3 Support decoding of text, mathematical notation, and symbols 2.4 Promote understanding across languages 2.5 Illustrate through multiple media	5: Provide options for expression and communication 5.1 Use multiple media for communication 5.2 Use multiple tools for construction and composition 5.3 Build fluencies with graduated levels of support for practice and performance	8: Provide options for sustaining effort and persistence 8.1 Heighten salience of goals and objectives 8.2 Vary demands and resources to optimize challenge 8.3 Foster collaboration and community 8.4 Increase mastery-oriented feedback
3: Provide options for comprehension 3.1 Activate or supply background knowledge 3.2. Highlight patterns, critical features, big ideas, and relationships 3.3 Guide information processing, visualization, and manipulation 3.4 Maximize transfer and generalization	6: Provide options for executive functions 6.1 Guide appropriate goal-setting 6.2 Support planning and strategy development 6.3 Facilitate managing information and resources 6.4 Enhance capacity for monitoring progress	9: Provide options for self-regulation 9.1 Promote expectations and beliefs that optimize motivation 9.2 Facilitate personal coping skills and strategies 9.3 Develop self-assessment and reflection

Source: CAST, 2011.

Figure 8.1: UDL guidelines.

What follows is a comparison between the UDL guidelines and the benefits learners get from playing digital and nondigital games and experiencing gameful design during the learning process. The UDL guidelines (CAST, 2011) appear in boxes throughout the chapter.

Multiple Means of Representation

1: Provide options for perception
1.1 Offer ways of customizing the display of information
1.2 Offer alternatives for auditory information
1.3 Offer alternatives for visual information

> Learners differ in the ways that they perceive and comprehend information that is presented to them. For example, those with sensory disabilities (e.g., blindness or deafness); learning disabilities (e.g., dyslexia); language or cultural differences, and so forth may all require different ways of approaching content. Others may simply grasp information quicker or more efficiently through visual or auditory means rather than printed text. Also learning, and transfer of learning, occurs when multiple representations are used because they allow students to make connections within, as well as between, concepts. In short, there is not one means of representation that will be optimal for all learners; providing options for representation is essential. (CAST, 2011)

Game developers understand that players must have information front and center—quickly and clearly communicated. Gaming requires players to make dozens of decisions every minute; therefore, information must be easy to access. Games also use symbology, rapid data communication methods (such as life meters, game statistics, and points), and capitalize on the reading habits of the digital generation (as described in chapter 2). Digital games provide visual information in an appealing and mesmerizing manner. And as digital gaming technology evolves, so do the visual elements of the game.

Games also relay audio information in different ways. They can include narration to provide information for players to use to advance the story line. Sound effects provide an authentic experience for players and help immerse them in gameplay. Finally, music and sound tracks accentuate gameplay, affecting players' moods and encouraging them to play on.

In the future, gaming systems will take advantage of new technologies such as *augmented reality* (technology that superimposes a digitally generated image on a user's real-world view). It will also include *virtual reality* (digital simulation of a three-dimensional image or environment) as well as *neuro gaming* (playing games with your brain) to better deliver visual and audio information to the brain and provide learners with diverse experiences as rich and robust as real life.

2: Provide options for language, mathematical expressions, and symbols
2.1 Clarify vocabulary and symbols
2.2 Clarify syntax and structure
2.3 Support decoding text, mathematical notation, and symbols
2.4 Promote understanding across languages
2.5 Illustrate through multiple media

Learners differ in how they obtain information—both linguistically and non-linguistically. Vocabulary and symbols that may sharpen and clarify concepts for one learner may be unclear or unknown to another. A picture or image that carries meaning for some learners may communicate very different meanings for others depending on their cultural background or life experiences. Inequalities may arise when information is presented to learners using one form of representation. An important instructional strategy is for educators to utilize alternative representations of information to add clarity and comprehensibility for all learners (CAST, 2011).

Video games are designed to provide universally understood information to a diverse population. Since gaming is now a global passion, many games support multiple languages, ages, and player abilities. Depending on the digital learning game, designers may incorporate images, text, audio narration, video, and a robust data interface. Players can receive a variety of information in different formats, so if one form of information is unclear, then alternate forms are available for clarification.

3: Provide options for comprehension
3.1 Activate or supply background knowledge
3.2 Highlight patterns, critical features, big ideas, and relationships
3.3 Guide information processing, visualization, and manipulation
3.4 Maximize transfer and generalization

The purpose of education is to guide learners to transform accessible information into usable knowledge. This process must be student centered and employ active learning strategies to acquire knowledge. Students must build new information upon their prior knowledge, memorize new content, learn new skills and processes, and transfer this new knowledge to relevant, real-world application.

Many digital games provide rich story lines to immerse players. These story lines often suspend reality and provide players with highly interactive virtual environments to experience. The story line provides or activates prior knowledge and highlights important or critical information. The player can take advantage of that knowledge just in time to make a right decision, answer a question or puzzle correctly, or save the day before re-entering reality. But perhaps the most important aspect of using digital games in the learning process is the transfer of learned or practiced content, skills, and processes to the real world.

Multiple Means of Action and Expression

4: Provide options for physical action
4.1 Vary the methods for response and navigation
4.2 Optimize access to tools and assistive technologies

> Properly designed curricular materials provide a seamless interface with common assistive technologies through which individuals with movement impairments can navigate and express what they know—to allow navigation or interaction with a single switch, through voice-activated switches, expanded keyboards and others. (CAST, 2011)

Players now have access to learning games on smartphones, tablets, laptops, gaming consoles, and portable gaming consoles. They have a variety of ways to control and manipulate gameplay. Tablets can be modified as assistive and adaptive technology tools for an intimate user interface. They are also very easy to navigate and control. Game consoles such as the Wii and Wii U by Nintendo and Xbox Kinect integrate motion and physical activity into video gameplay. Players are no longer required to sit down and try to touch eight buttons or manipulate three joysticks. The interaction between gamer and game is becoming easier and more natural than in the past, leaving no person out of the gaming experience based on ability or disability.

5: Provide options for expression and communication
5.1 Use multiple media for communication
5.2 Use multiple tools for construction and composition
5.3 Build fluencies with graduated levels of support for practice and performance

It is important for educators to provide numerous modalities for expression, both to level the playing field among learners and to allow the learner to appropriately express ideas and concepts in the classroom (CAST, 2011). Consuming and creating media is a valuable way for students to acquire knowledge and demonstrate their mastery of that knowledge. Students can learn from media such as text passages, audio clips, lectures, images, video segments, music, hypertext, simulations, and digital games. They are also able to create or compose media to demonstrate their understanding.

Digital games are so popular because they are immersive, engaging, and tell intricate stories with interesting characters. But they also help players become better with built-in assistance. In-game clues, narration, callouts, symbols, and the need to fail and try again are just some of the features that digital learning games have to scaffold the learning process for players.

6: Provide options for executive functions
6.1 Guide appropriate goal-setting
6.2 Support planning and strategy development
6.3 Facilitate managing information and resources
6.4 Enhance capacity for monitoring progress

Executive functions are the capabilities that "allow humans to overcome impulsive, short-term reactions to their environment and instead to set long-term goals, plan effective strategies for reaching those goals, monitor their progress, and modify strategies as needed" (CAST, 2011).

Digital games are environments where players are constantly setting and achieving both short- and long-term goals to progress in gameplay. The components and mechanics of the game, such as winning a level, unlocking new virtual achievements, earning points, or ascending the leaderboard help propel players to persevere and achieve their goals.

Most video games require players to plan and strategize to advance in the story line or experience. A well-constructed game requires players to manage and use virtual resources wisely, or they will not proceed to the next level or win. Digital games provide players with constant incentives, rewards, and feedback, which appeals to the executive functions of the brain.

Multiple Means of Engagement

7: Provide options for recruiting interest
7.1 Optimize individual choice and autonomy
7.2 Optimize relevance, value, and authenticity
7.3 Minimize threats and distractions

> Learners differ significantly in terms of what attracts their atten-
> tion and engages their interest. Even the same learner will differ
> over time and circumstance; their "interests" change as they
> develop and gain new knowledge and skills, as their biological
> environments change, and as they develop into self-determined
> adolescents and adults. It is, therefore, important to have alter-
> native ways to recruit learner interest, ways that reflect the
> important inter- and intra-individual differences amongst learn-
> ers. (CAST, 2011)

Digital games, like a good book or movie, can draw players in with a great story line. The number of subscribers to *World of Warcraft* has fluctuated significantly over the past few years—from between 6 to 10 million players. The reason for this drastic fluctuation coincides with the release of a new expansion pack, which freshens the story line and gameplay (Statistica, 2015b). With thousands of game developers creating tens of thousands of games annually, gamers have their choice to select the games they wish to play and learn at the same time. If a person is interested in history, then he or she can select from *Age of Empires*, *Medal of Honor: Allied Assault*, *Mayan Mysteries*, and *The Oregon Trail* to name a few. If his or her interests involve science, then *The Cure*, *Spore*, and *Science4Us* are good choices.

Many digital learning games have depth and purpose that transcend entertain-ment. Within their story lines and gameplay are simulated problems for players to solve—the same type of authentic problems they must contend with in real life. There are digital games that challenge players to balance a checkbook, keep a plant alive, map the human genome, and solve fictitious crimes using foren-sic science. Disguised as entertainment, games promote learning through play. Finally, if the gamer fails or loses, then he or she simply starts over and tries again.

Digital learning games allow players to fail and learn from their mistakes. And this failure does not carry the same burden as failing a test in schools. The player learns, adapts, tries again, and moves on to the next challenge.

8: Provide options for sustaining effort and persistence

8.1 Heighten salience of goals and objectives

8.2 Vary demands and resources to optimize challenge

8.3 Foster collaboration and community

8.4 Increase mastery-oriented feedback

> Many kinds of learning require sustained attention and effort, especially when a learner is exploring new skills and strategies. Motivated learners can regulate their attention and affect to sustain the effort and concentration that such learning will require. (CAST, 2011)

The components of a digital game keep the player challenged. Rules, time limits, challenges, points, level objectives, and positive and negative feedback are all integrated into the gameplay to progress the player. Digital games also assist players in succeeding by offering them in-game scaffolding. This scaffolding could be in the form of clues, story lines, new virtual tools or abilities, or other virtual elements that assist the players to win just in time. As digital learning games continue to evolve, there are more opportunities to collaborate and compete with other players so they can master any challenge thrown their way.

9: Provide options for self-regulation

9.1 Promote expectations and beliefs that optimize motivation

9.2 Facilitate personal coping skills and strategies

9.3 Develop self-assessment and reflection

Although games help players address the extrinsic factors such as resources, the learning environment, and social interaction, they also help players develop their intrinsic abilities to self-regulate and control their emotional state. Games of any sort are inclined to force the player to reflect on his or her performance to hopefully improve in the future.

Gamers become better at gameplay through practice, repetition, and personal reflection. When they first start playing, gamers often fail or perform poorly. However, as they play more, they become better through trial and error. Gamers also expect this challenge. If a game is too easy, then they will bore with it quickly and move on to a new activity. Good digital learning games are the ones that operate right on the verge of being too difficult. So once a player achieves success, he or she assesses his or her own performance, reflects upon it, and uses this newly acquired knowledge for the next digital or nondigital challenge he or she faces.

Universal Design for Learning is not the only framework educators can use to compare the learning attributes present in play-based learning, digital game–based learning, and gamification. Educational gaming can be linked to Bloom's taxonomy (1956) and its hierarchy of thinking skills. The assistance and scaffolding digital games provide to players can also be aligned to Vygotsky's *zone of proximal development*, which is the "distance between the actual developmental level as determined by independent problem solving and the level of potential development as determined through problem solving under adult guidance, or in collaboration with more capable peers" (Vygotsky, 1978, p. 86). Play and digital game–based learning can also be linked to John Dewey's theory of experiential learning. Dewey (1933) believes that past knowledge and experiences build new knowledge.

Games, both digital and nondigital, are rich in experience and context. They allow students to call upon their past experiences to play better. Games are not just child's play. They are versatile and immersive tools educators can use to support, develop, and nurture learners, which are key ingredients for academic success.

Summarizing the Main Points

- Architects have embraced universal design as a philosophy to meet the needs of all users.

- Universal Design for Learning principles offer everyone access, not just people with special needs.

- Educators are beginning to embrace these principles when designing and delivering instruction to diverse learning populations.

- Digital games, gamification, and play-based learning in the classroom connect with many of the UDL guidelines.

Questions to Consider

1. Why does the philosophy of universal design transfer to learning with such ease?

2. After scanning the UDL guidelines, are there indicators that you adapt for your lessons already? Are there other guidelines to consider during the planning and implementation process of a lesson?

3. How do digital games, gamification, and play offer options in perception, language, and comprehension of information or data?

4. How do digital games, gamification, and play offer options in action, expression, and communication?

5. How do digital games, gamification, and play offer options in self-regulation, preserving interest, and encouraging persistence and effort?

Chapter 9

Beyond Linear Presentations

If you get stuck, draw with a different pen. Change your tools; it may free your thinking.

—Paul Arden

Despite the thousands of digital games on the market, not every concept, skill, or instructional unit will have a corresponding game for teachers to use with their students. Sometimes educators must use their own creativity and resourcefulness to create just the right digital game. Although Microsoft PowerPoint is widely embraced as presentation software, educators have found new and creative ways to refashion this readily available slideshow program for digital gaming. For example, it can imitate the games *Jeopardy!* and *Who Wants to Be a Millionaire?* online or at a professional workshop. These are just two examples of how to use a program like PowerPoint for digital gaming in the classroom. This chapter explores other options to engage readers.

Using PowerPoint for Digital Gaming

Teachers often use PowerPoint as a linear presentation tool. The slideshow progresses one slide at a time from the first slide to the last. Figure 9.1 (page 116) shows a typical linear PowerPoint presentation.

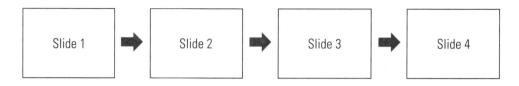

Figure 9.1: Diagram of a linear PowerPoint slideshow.

However, PowerPoint can function far beyond a linear presentation tool. (See figure 9.2.) When the PowerPoint presentation is designed to be navigated in a nonlinear manner, the viewer can select his or her own path through the presentation. Teachers can add hyperlinks, links to other files or slides, and action buttons to create a divergent experience.

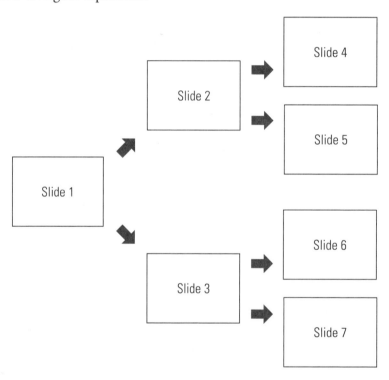

Figure 9.2: Diagram of a nonlinear PowerPoint slideshow.

Nonlinear PowerPoints allow viewers to become active participants, because they control the flow of the slideshow. In the past, teachers used nonlinear PowerPoints with their students for storyboarding, delivering webquests, and creating or reading digital books. They can also structure a nonlinear PowerPoint into a game.

Creating a Game in PowerPoint

Following is a step-by-step guide for creating your own game using PowerPoint. It is important to note that there are numerous versions of Microsoft PowerPoint, so the following directions may differ slightly from version to version; however, teachers can embed most of the features into a nonlinear game.

Identifying the Purpose of the Game and Creating a Game Structure

When creating a game, it's important for teachers to identify the game's purpose. Will it teach or assess students? What content will the game cover? Next, educators must think of a simple story line or game structure to frame the game-based learning experience for players. (See chapter 10 on takeaways [page 123] and the Evernote public notebook [http://bit.ly/GamingEvernote] for specific examples of PowerPoint games.) Consider how players will engage with the game. For example, will they select an answer, choose a story line option, or discuss the options as a team?

Adding Text

To insert text onto slides, simply click inside a textbox and start typing. The game designer can always add text boxes by going to the Insert > Textbox command.

Inserting Links

To insert links into the PowerPoint game, follow these steps.

1. Type and highlight the word or words or object that will be the link.

2. Go to Insert > Hyperlink.

3. Indicate what slide (anchor) or web address will be the link's destination.

In figure 9.3 (page 118), the game designer is programming a link to navigate to a different slide.

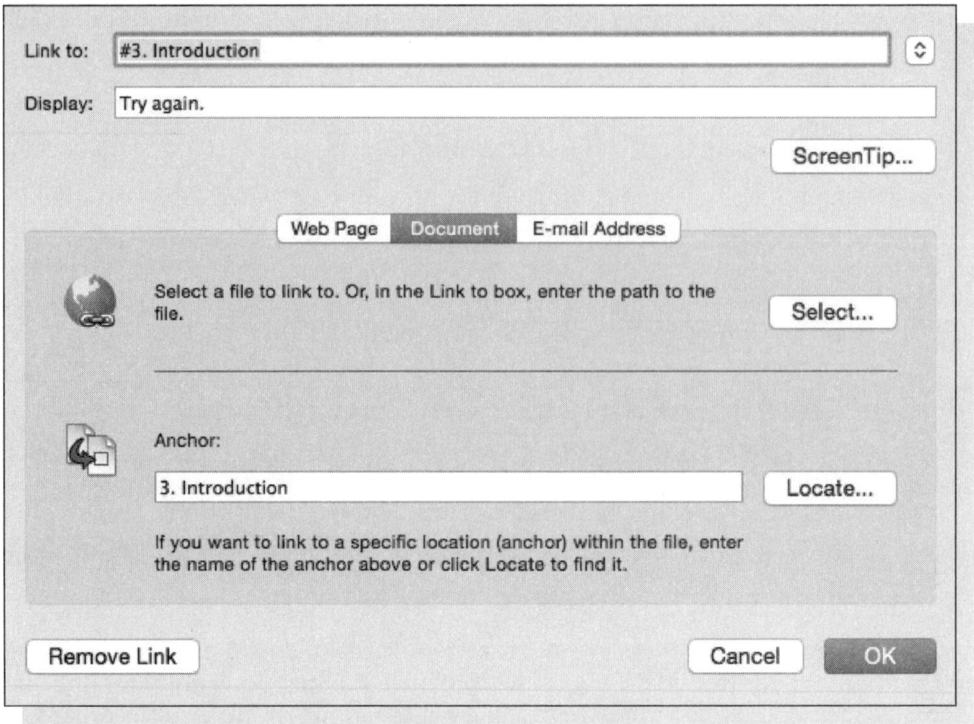

Source: PowerPoint® presentation graphics program. Used with permission from Microsoft.

Figure 9.3: Inserting link to a slide in PowerPoint.

Inserting Action Buttons

Custom action buttons allow players to progress through the game to a predetermined slide. Many of the buttons use universal symbols, such as for Next slide, Previous slide, and Sound, which allows players to navigate through the game easier. There are options within PowerPoint to use premade action buttons or create custom action buttons. To insert a premade action button:

• Go to Slide Show > Action Buttons > Choose the desired button.

See figure 9.4 for a list of the potential action buttons game designers can add in their nonlinear PowerPoints.

To create custom action buttons, select the custom button option. A blank rectangle button will appear. Teachers can add text to the button, and an action menu will appear and program what action the button will perform. See figure 9.5 (page 120) for a visual of the different options game designers have for action buttons.

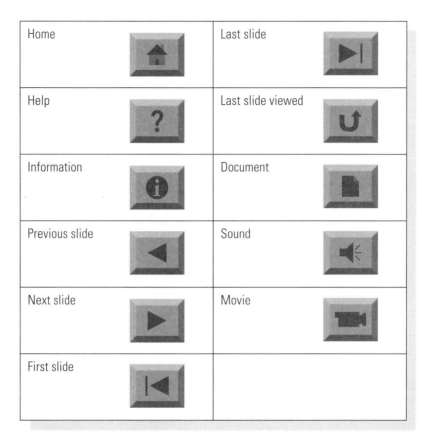

Source: PowerPoint® presentation graphics program. Used with permission from Microsoft.

Figure 9.4: Premade action buttons in PowerPoint.

Disabling Advance on Mouse-Click Feature

PowerPoint allows users to advance slides on a mouse click. Although it is convenient for a person creating and delivering a presentation, it is a function that might spoil gameplay. For slides that require player interaction, it is prudent to disable the mouse-click feature.

- Go to Slide Show > Transitions > Uncheck Advance on Mouse Click.

This must be done for each slide to prevent an accidental slide progression.

If you are having difficulty programming your game, consult the Help menu or explore how-to videos on YouTube for guidance.

Source: PowerPoint® presentation graphics program. Used with permission from Microsoft.

Figure 9.5: Programming custom buttons in PowerPoint.

Finding Examples of Nonlinear PowerPoint Games

Please consult chapter 10 (page 123) for directions on finding game examples or visit http://bit.ly/GamingEvernote and find the nonlinear PowerPoint note to download and view these files.

Playing *Pitfall Pete*: A Nonlinear PowerPoint Game

Pitfall is a classic game for Atari 2600 (Crane, 1982). During gameplay, the main character, Pete, runs around the game screen jumping over fire, snakes, crocodiles, and quicksand in his search for gold. *Pitfall Pete* is a nonlinear PowerPoint game inspired by the Atari game story line of an adventurer on an expedition. The game teaches and assesses scenarios exploring cause and effect, while simultaneously allowing students to research Africa and survival skills. Learners start at the beginning of the game with directions and a reading passage to set up the story line and introduce the relationship between cause and effect. See figure 9.6 to see the *Pitfall Pete* slideshow story line with links to the answer slides.

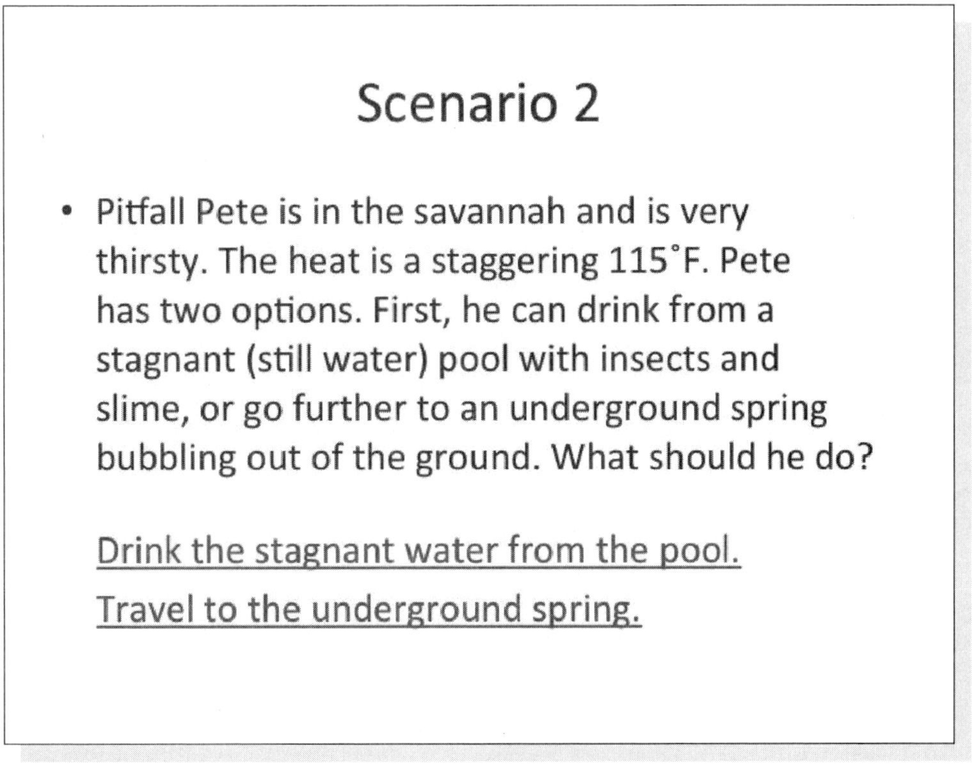

Scenario 2

- Pitfall Pete is in the savannah and is very thirsty. The heat is a staggering 115°F. Pete has two options. First, he can drink from a stagnant (still water) pool with insects and slime, or go further to an underground spring bubbling out of the ground. What should he do?

Drink the stagnant water from the pool.
Travel to the underground spring.

Figure 9.6: Question from *Pitfall Pete* gameplay.

Students experience each scenario and make a choice. If the choice is correct, they progress to the next scenario. If their decision is wrong, they land on a Game Over slide and start the adventure over with Pete. This structure allows players to fail and learn with the game. The structure of *Pitfall Pete* is fairly simple, due in part because the content is meant for third-graders. Nonlinear PowerPoints are easy to customize and can be more complex for older students or simpler for younger students. Educators can create PowerPoint games in any subject area.

Using Different Slideshow Versions and Programs

We selected the PowerPoint program as a tool for creating nonlinear games because of its prevalence in schools and businesses. Apple's Keynote software is very similar in function and can be programmed in a nonlinear manner. Google's online slideshow program, *Slides*, can also be structured using many of the same methods examined here using PowerPoint.

Summarizing the Main Points

- Slideshows do not have to be structured in a linear manner.

- When PowerPoint is used to design a presentation to be navigated in a nonlinear manner, the viewer becomes a player as he or she selects a path through the presentation.

- Nonlinear PowerPoint games allow learners to navigate through a story by clicking on action buttons to progress.

Questions to Consider

1. What nonlinear PowerPoint game ideas do you have?
2. How will you design the game to be interactive for your students?

Chapter 10
Takeaways

Game-based learning and gamification are gaining popularity and generating serious buzz in the education world. Despite the significant surge in interest, educators are often left in search of support and ideas for implementing digital games in their classrooms. This chapter provides three takeaway tools—(1) a list of education blogs, (2) an Evernote public notebook, and (3) the Digital Learning Game Database—educators can use as they embark on the journey of implementing gaming experiences with their students.

Takeaway 1: Education Super Blogs

The following are five of the best education blogs that often publish insightful articles about gaming and digital learning.

Edudemic

The goal of *Edudemic* (www.edudemic.com) is to connect teachers, administrators, students, and just about everyone else with the best technology on the planet. It has grown to become one of the leading education technology websites. It's become a vibrant forum for discussion, discovery, and knowledge. The site features a regular flow of tools, tips, resources, visuals, and guest posts from dozens of authors around the world.

Edutopia

Edutopia (www.edutopia.org) shares cutting-edge classroom practices about project-based learning, student teams working cooperatively, students connecting with content experts, and broad forms of assessment. It also focuses on new digital multimedia and telecommunications that can support these practices and engage students in meaningful and relevant learning experiences.

InfoSavvy21

InfoSavvy21's blog (http://infosavvy21.com/blog) examines everything associated with teaching the digital generation using cutting-edge practices. This site features teaching strategies, tools, resources, and posts from numerous authors.

MindShift

MindShift (https://ww2.kqed.org/mindshift/) explores the many dimensions of learning, including cultural and technology trends, innovations in education, research, education policy, and more.

TeachThought

TeachThought (www.teachthought.com) supports K–12 educators in evolving learning for 21st century students. Its primary interest is exploring emerging learning models, such as blended learning, project-based learning, and self-directed learning, while simultaneously exploring the role of play in learning and supporting educators' professional development.

Takeaway 2: Evernote Public Notebook

Evernote, a free app, is an excellent resource to collect and curate web content, journal articles, and research studies associated with digital gaming and learning. Visit http://bit.ly/GamingEvernote to access a dynamic database of digital-gaming materials and resources. With over one hundred pages of content (and pages added daily), the Evernote notebook is like purchasing a supplemental text.

Takeaway 3: Digital Learning Game Database

In a joint effort among seasoned educators, the InfoSavvy21 team collaborated to create the Digital Learning Game Database (DLGD; http://bit.ly/DigitalLearningGameDatabase). It archives and curates digital games with learning potential for educators to use with their students. One of the biggest barriers to incorporating digital games into lessons is the struggle involved with finding good games for deep, immersive learning. The database's entries are alphabetized and note the subject area, with summaries of the game and concept and skills tags to identify what the game helps to teach or test. The games are also categorized by gaming platform, such as web based, desktop, console, or mobile (like Apple iOS and Google Play). The DLGD has hundreds of games for visitors to search through and is constantly growing with new games added daily to help facilitators deliver quality digital game–based learning experiences to their students. Figure 10.1 shows a page from the database.

Digital Learning Game Database

Game Title	Thumbnail	Platform	URL Source	Game Description	Subject(s)	Concept Tags
2048		iOS	https://itunes.apple.c om/us/app/2048/id8 40919914?mt=8	Players move numbered tile to make matches. Numbers will double until you either reach 2048 or there are no longer any turns left.	Mathematics	addition, doubles
3rd World Farmer		Web Browser-Based	http://3rdworldfarmer.c om/	3rd World Farmer is a serious-thought-provoking online game and business strategy simulation activity where you have to manage an impoverished farm. In 3rd World Farmer, you have to make tough moral and survival decisions in order to provide for your underprivileged family, while enduring droughts, disease, poverty, corruption and war.	Mathematics, Social Studies	Economics, Poverty, Business Strategy, Business Management, Opportunity Costs, Survival Skills, Problem Solving, Morals, Social Studies, Developing Countries
Addimal Adventure		iOS	https://itunes.apple.c om/us/app/teachley-addimal-adventure/i d661286973?mt=8	Addimal Adventure is an excellent tool for teaching kids strategies they need to master single-digit addition	Mathematics	Addition

Source: Courtesy of Becky Koza, Ryan Schaaf, & InfoSavvy21.

Figure 10.1: Digital Learning Game Database.

Crowdsourcing is a powerful phenomenon in the digital age. The DLGD takes advantage of this phenomenon as well. *Crowdsourcing* allows people to band together to perform incredible acts of productivity and altruism. The perfect example of the power of crowdsourcing and social media is the ALS (amyotrophic lateral sclerosis) Association Ice Bucket Challenge. During the challenge, participants spread ALS awareness by donating $100 million to fund research and clinical-management projects to combat the disease. Each participant performed a simple stunt (dumping a bucket of ice water over his or her head) and shared it on social networking sites such as Facebook and Instagram.

The ALS Ice Bucket Challenge took advantage of the participatory nature of digital culture. It was a litmus test to prove the existence of a powerful social fabric created from our need to connect. We can use this same power to crowdsource a new tool to help educators find the digital games they need for powerful and immersive learning with digital learners. When educators find digital games that other educators could use with their students, they can go to the online form on DLGD (http://bit.ly/DLGDEntryForm) to add it to the extensive list of games. Those who add games are participating in creating a powerful resource for educators who are interested in finding games to use in their classrooms. New games are reviewed (by the authors) and then added to the ever-growing resource list.

The Right Balance

Using games during the learning and assessment process can add high levels of motivation, engagement, and fun for learners. The number of digital games will no doubt continue to grow, their quality and design will improve on a daily basis, and more and more people will adopt gaming as a pastime. As for the field of education, digital game–based learning and gameful design experiences will continue to seep into the cultures of our schools as more educators realize their awesome potential. A word of caution—digital games should never be over-utilized in schools. If used too often, they will lose their appeal for both students and teachers. Instead, educational gaming should become another approach for educators to consider adding to their toolbox of teaching strategies—pulled out at the right time in the learning. Balance is an attribute the always-on generation lacks at times. As parents and educators, we must help students maintain a balance between digital and nondigital experiences.

Today's educators must find common ground with the digital generation to reach students in the classroom. With the stress of testing, accountability, and new initiatives, educators' jobs are more challenging than ever before. However, embracing new approaches—especially ones that are fun and intellectually stimulating to students—is an easy choice to make. To the teachers of today and tomorrow: game on with your students!

REFERENCES AND RESOURCES

Anderson, L. W., & Krathwohl, D. (Eds.). (2001). *A taxonomy for learning, teaching, and assessing: A revision of Bloom's taxonomy of educational objectives.* New York: Longman.

AppBrain. (2014). *Top 10 Google Play categories.* Accessed at www.appbrain.com/stats /android-market-app-categories on January 9, 2015.

Badkar, M. (2010). The 8 biggest video game releases ever. *Business Insider.* Accessed at www.businessinsider.com/biggest-video-game-releases-2010-11 on May 20, 2015.

Barros, R. M., Silver, E. J., & Stein, R. E. K. (2009). School recess and group classroom behavior. *Pediatrics, 123*(2), 431–436.

Beavis, C. (2012). Video games in the classroom: Developing digital literacies. *Practically Primary, 17*(1), 17–20. Accessed at www.alea.edu.au/documents/item/355 on January 9, 2015.

Blanchard, O. (2010, May 20). *10 things Julius Caesar could have taught us about business, marketing, leadership (and even social media)* [Blog post]. Accessed at https:// thebrandbuilder.wordpress.com/2010/05/20/10-things-julius-caesar-could-have-taught -us-about-business-marketing-leadership-and-even-social-media on February 16, 2015.

Bligh, D. A. (2000). *What's the use of lectures?* San Francisco: Jossey-Bass.

Blikstein, P. (2013). *Seymour Papert's legacy: Thinking about learning, and learning about thinking.* Stanford, CA: Transformative Learning Technologies Lab, Stanford Graduate School of Education. Accessed at https://tltl.stanford.edu/content/seymour-papert-s -legacy-thinking-about-learning-and-learning-about-thinking on January 9, 2015.

Bloom, B. S. (Ed.). (1956). *Taxonomy of educational objectives, handbook I: Cognitive domain.* New York: McKay.

Bodrova, E., & Leong, D. (2015). Vygotskian and Post-Vygotskian views on children's play. *American Journal of Play, 7*(3), 371–388.

Borden, J. (2015). Education 3.0: Embracing technology to 'jump the curve.' *Wired*. Accessed at www.wired.com/insights/2013/09/education-3-0-embracing-technology -to-jump-the-curve on November 1, 2015.

Bronkhorst, Q. (2012). Games vs. movies: Who wins? *BusinessTech*. Accessed at http:// businesstech.co.za/news/general/19901/games-vs-movies-who-wins on August 25, 2015.

Burke, B. (2013). The gamification of business. *Forbes*. Accessed at www.forbes.com /sites/gartnergroup/2013/01/21/the-gamification-of-business on May 20, 2015.

Carpenter, K., Pager, D., & Labrecque, R. (2013, August). *Teachley: Addimal Adventure— Bridging research and technology to help children foster strategy development, conceptual understanding, and number fact fluency* [White paper]. Accessed at www.teachley.com /assets/docs/White-Paper-Addimal-Adventure.pdf on January 9, 2015.

Carpenter, S. K., Pashler, H., Cepeda, N. J., & Alvarez, D. (2007). Applying the principles of testing and spacing to classroom learning. In D. S. McNamara & J. G. Trafton (Eds.), *Proceedings of the 29th Annual Cognitive Science Society* (pp. 19–20). Nashville, TN: Cognitive Science Society.

Center for Applied Special Technology. (2011). *Universal Design for Learning guidelines version 2.0*. Wakefield, MA: Author.

Chou, Y-K. (2013). *Top 10 marketing gamification cases you won't forget*. Accessed at www.yukaichou.com/gamification-examples/top-10-marketing-gamification-cases -remember/#.VOI9zbDF-4Q on February 16, 2015.

Classcraft. (2015). *About*. Accessed at www.classcraft.com/about on August 25, 2015.

Cooper, M. (2011). The pedagogy of gaming. *W Columns*. Accessed at www.washington .edu/alumni/columns-magazine/march-2011/features/pedagogy on August 25, 2015.

Costa, A. L., & Kallick, B. (Eds.). (2000). *Discovering & exploring the habits of mind*. Alexandria, VA: Association for Supervision and Curriculum Development.

Crane, D. (1982). *Pitfall!* [Video game]. Santa Monica, CA: Activision.

Dale, E. (1969). *Audiovisual methods in teaching* (3rd ed.). New York: Dryden Press.

Derosier, M. (2014). Game-based social skills assessments: Making the play for better emotional health. *EmergingEdTech*. Accessed at www.emergingedtech.com/2014/07 /game-based-social-skills-assessments on January 9, 2015.

Dewey, J. (1933). *How we think: A restatement of the relation of reflective thinking to the educative process*. Boston: Heath.

Diele, O. (2013). *2013 State of Online Gaming Report*. Hilversum, The Netherlands: Spil Games. Accessed at http://auth-83051f68-ec6c-44e0-afe5-bd8902acff57.cdn .spilcloud.com/v1/archives/1384952861.25_State_of_Gaming_2013_US_FINAL .pdf on January 9, 2015.

Dybwad, B. (2010). Nintendo DS enters schools in Japan this fall. *Mashable*. Accessed at http://mashable.com/2010/03/22/nintendo-ds-enters-japanese-schools on August 25, 2015.

Entertainment Software Association. (2013). *2013 sales, demographic and usage data: Essential facts about the computer and video game industry*. Accessed at www.isfe.eu /sites/isfe.eu/files/attachments/esa_ef_2013.pdf on August 25, 2015.

Entertainment Software Association. (2014). *Games: Improving education*. Accessed at www.theesa.com/wp-content/uploads/2014/11/Games_Improving_Education -11.4.pdf on February 16, 2015.

Entertainment Software Association. (2015). *2015 sales, demographic and usage data: Essential facts about the computer and video game industry*. Accessed at www.theesa .com/wp-content/uploads/2015/04/ESA-Essential-Facts-2015.pdf on May 20, 2016.

Entertainment Software Association. (2016). *2016 sales, demographic and usage data: Essential facts about the computer and video game industry*. Accessed at http:// essentialfacts.theesa.com/Essential-Facts-2016.pdf on July 20, 2016.

Evans, B. (2011, November 23). *National STEM video game challenge open for students and educators* [Blog post]. Accessed at www.whitehouse.gov/blog/2011/11/23 /national-stem-video-game-challenge-open-students-and-educators on July 25, 2015.

Fishman, B., Riconscente, M., Snider, R., Tsai, T., & Plass, J. (2014). *Empowering educators: Supporting student progress in the classroom with digital games—Part 1: A national survey examining teachers' digital game use and formative assessment practices*. Ann Arbor: University of Michigan. Accessed at http://gamesandlearning.umich.edu/wp-content /uploads/2014/11/A-GAMES-Part-I_A-National-Survey.pdf on January 13, 2015.

Freeman, S., Eddy, S. L., McDonough, M., Smith, M. K., Okoroafor, N., Jordt, H., et al. (2014). Active learning increases student performance in science, engineering, and mathematics. *Proceedings of the National Academy of Sciences of the United States of America, 111*(23), 8410–8415. Accessed at www.pnas.org/content/111/23/8410 .abstract?tab=author-info on January 26, 2016.

Frum, L. (2013). *Nearly half of all video-gamers are women*. Accessed at www.cnn .com/2013/08/08/tech/gaming-gadgets/female-gamers on May 20, 2015.

Galarneau, L. (2014, January 16). *2014 global gaming stats: Who's playing what, and why?* [Blog post]. Accessed at www.bigfishgames.com/blog/2014-global-gaming-stats-whos -playing-what-and-why on August 25, 2015.

Games for Change. (2015). *About*. Accessed at www.gamesforchange.org/about on January 23, 2015.

Gartner. (2013). *Gartner says worldwide video game market to total $93 billion in 2013* [Press release]. Accessed at www.gartner.com/newsroom/id/2614915 on July 20, 2016.

Gee, J. P. (2007). *Good video games and good learning: Collected essays on video games, learning, and literacy*. New York: Lang.

Gee, J. P., & Shaffer, D. W. (2010, April). *Looking where the light is bad: Video games and the future of assessment* (Epistemic Games Group Working Paper No. 2010–02). Accessed at http://edgaps.org/gaps/wp-content/uploads/Looking-where-the-light-is -bad-tr1.pdf on January 26, 2016.

Giedd, J. N. (2015). The amazing teen brain: Rapidly changing wiring leads to mental agility—and risky behavior. *Scientific American, 312*(6), 33–37.

Glasser, W. (1986). *Control theory in the classroom*. New York: Perennial Library.

Green, C. S., & Bavelier, D. (2003). Action video game modifies visual selective attention. *Nature, 423*, 534–537.

Green, C. S., & Bavelier, D. (2007). Action-video-game experience alters the spatial resolution of vision. *Psychological Science, 18*(1), 88–94.

Hearn, M., & Winner, M. C. (2013). *Teach math with the Wii: Engage your K–7 students through gaming technology*. Eugene, OR: International Society for Technology in Education.

Hembree, R. (2012). Correlates, causes, effects, and treatment of test anxiety. *Review of Educational Research, 58*(1), 47–77.

Horn, M. (2014). KAIST doesn't wait for change in Korea, pioneers "Education 3.0." *Forbes*. Accessed at www.forbes.com/sites/michaelhorn/2014/03/17/kaist-doesnt -wait-for-change-in-korea-pioneers-education-3-0 on November 1, 2015.

Hort-Francis, A. (2014, May 30). *BA6 essay—Is the serious game movement detrimental to the development of digital games?* [Blog post]. Accessed at https://hortfrancisblog .wordpress.com/2014/05/30/ba6-essay-is-the-serious-games-movement-detrimental -to-the-development-of-digital-games on August 25, 2015.

Hsu, J. (2010). For the U.S. Military, video games get serious. *Live Science*. Accessed at www.livescience.com/10022-military-video-games.html on July 15, 2016.

Huang, T-T., & Plass, J. L. (2009). *Microsoft research: Games for Learning Institute— History of play in education* [White paper]. New York: Games for Learning Institute. Accessed at http://g4li.org/wp-content/uploads/2009/10/6-History-of-Play.pdf on January 13, 2015.

Hugos, M. (2012). Games and business have much in common. *Forbes*. Accessed at www.forbes.com/sites/oreillymedia/2012/11/28/games-and-businesses-have-much -in-common on July 25, 2015.

Hymes, J. L., Jr. (2010). *Your child's potential—Promote it through play*. Accessed at www .preschools.coop/v/your-childs-potential on May 20, 2015.

Institute of Play. (2014). *GlassLab*. Accessed at www.instituteofplay.org/work/projects /glasslab on January 9, 2015.

International Education Advisory Board. (n.d.). *Learning in the 21st century: Teaching today's students on their terms.* Accessed at www.certiport.com/Portal/Common /DocumentLibrary/IEAB_Whitepaper040808.pdf on August 4, 2016.

International Society for Technology in Education. (2007). *ISTE standards for students.* Accessed at www.iste.org/standards/ISTE-standards/standards-for-students on May 10, 2016.

Ivec, S. (2013). *How e-Learning games translate into real-world success.* Accessed at http:// elearningindustry.com/how-e-learning-games-translate-into-real-world-success on July 25, 2015.

Jacobs, P. (2014). Here's why a controversial plan to give an iPad to every Los Angeles public school student failed. *Business Insider.* Accessed at www.businessinsider.com /why-controversial-plan-to-give-ipads-to-la-public-school-students-failed-2014-10 on May 20, 2015.

Jensen, E. (2008). *Brain-based learning* (2nd ed.). Thousand Oaks, CA: Corwin Press.

Johnson, L., Adams, S., & Cummins, M. (2012). *NMC Horizon report: 2012 K–12 edition.* Austin, TX: New Media Consortium.

Johnson, L., Adams, S., & Haywood, K. (2011). *NMC Horizon report: 2011 K–12 edition.* Austin, TX: New Media Consortium.

Johnson, L., Becker, S. A., Cummins, M., Estrada, V., Freeman, A., & Ludgate, H. (2013). *NMC Horizon report: 2013 higher education edition.* Austin, TX: New Media Consortium.

Johnson, L., Becker, S. A., Estrada, V., & Freeman, A. (2014). *NMC Horizon report: 2014 K–12 edition.* Austin, TX: New Media Consortium.

Johnson, L., Smith, R., Levine, A., & Haywood, K. (2010). *2010 Horizon report: K–12 edition.* Austin, TX: New Media Consortium.

Jukes, I., McCain, T., & Crockett, L. (2010). *Understanding the digital generation: Teaching and learning in the new digital landscape.* Seattle, WA: CreateSpace Independent Publishing Platform.

Jukes, I., Schaaf, R. L., & Mohan, N. (2015). *Reinventing learning for the always-on generation: Srategies and apps that work.* Bloomington, IN: Solution Tree Press.

Kamenetz, A. (2013). *Why video games succeed where the movie and music industries fail.* Accessed at www.fastcompany.com/3021008/why-video-games-succeed-where-the -movie-and-music-industries-fail on August 25, 2015.

Kane, A., & Meyers, G. (2010). *Virtual pig: Pfizer's animal health 3-D serious game.* Accessed at www.elearningguild.com/olf/olfarchives/index.cfm?id=712&action =viewonly on February 16, 2015.

Kapp, K. M. (2012). *The gamification of learning and instruction: Game-based methods and strategies for training and education.* San Francisco: Pfeiffer.

Kapp, K. (2013). *Testing games vs. teaching games.* Accessed at http://karlkapp.com /testing-games-vs-teaching-games on January 9, 2015.

Kennedy, A., & Barblett, L. (2010). *Learning and teaching through play: Supporting the Early Years Learning Framework.* Accessed at www.earlychildhoodaustralia.org .au/nqsplp/wp-content/uploads/2012/05/RIP1003-EYLF_sample.pdf on August 1, 2016.

Klopfer, E. (2008). *Augmented learning: Research and design of mobile educational games.* Cambridge, MA: MIT Press.

Korbey, H. (2014, June 9). *Surprising insights: How teachers use games in the classroom* [Blog post]. Accessed at http://blogs.kqed.org/mindshift/2014/06/surprising-insights -how-teachers-use-games-in-the-classroom on January 9, 2015.

Kovach, S. (2014). Tim Cook had a really interesting answer for why iPad sales appear to be stalling. *Business Insider.* Accessed at www.businessinsider.com/tim-cook-ipad -sales-2014-4 on May 20, 2015.

Lang, D. (2012). Ray Bradbury retrospective. *USA Today.* Accessed at http:// usatoday30.usatoday.com/life/books/news/story/2012-06-06/ray-bradbury -appreciation/55424240/1 on July, 15, 2016.

Lengel, J. (2013). *Education 3.0: Seven steps to better schools.* New York: Teachers College Press.

Lenhart, A., Jones, S., & Macgill, A. (2008). *Adults and video games.* Washington, DC: Pew Research Center. Accessed at www.pewinternet.org/2008/12/07/adults-and -video-games on May 20, 2015.

Lenhart, A., Kahne, J., Middaugh, E., Macgill, A., Evans, C., & Vitak, J. (2008). *Teens, video games and civics.* Washington, DC: Pew Research Center. Accessed at http:// pewinternet.org/Reports/2008/Teens-Video-Games-and-Civics.aspx on May 20, 2015.

Lombardi, M. (2007). Authentic learning for the 21st century: An overview. *Educause Learning Initiative.* Accessed at https://net.educause.edu/ir/library/pdf/ELI3009.pdf on August 1, 2016.

Lopez, M. (2014). *Gamification: The key to re-engaging high school dropouts.* Accessed at www.lawyerment.com/library/articles/Reference_and_Education/Higher _Education/6246.htm on January 26, 2016.

Malhoit, L. (2012, August 28). *Cisco Aspire game helps CCNA training* [Blog post]. Accessed at www.techrepublic.com/blog/career-management/cisco-aspire-game-helps -ccna-training on February 16, 2015.

Martone, A., & Sireci, S. (2009). Evaluating alignment between curriculum, assessment, and instruction. *Review of Educational Research.* Accessed at http://rer.sagepub.com/ content/79/4/1332.abstract on August 6, 2016.

Maryland State Department of Education. (2016). *Using the state curriculum: Government, high school; economics.* Accessed at http://mdk12.msde.maryland.gov/instruction/hsvsc /government/standard4.html on October 12, 2016.

Maslow, A. (1943). A theory of human motivation. *Psychological Review, 50,* 370–396.

McCain, T. (2015). *Teaching with the future in mind.* Unpublished manuscript.

McGonigal, J. (2010). *Jane McGonigal: Gaming can make a better world* [Video file]. Accessed at www.ted.com/talks/jane_mcgonigal_gaming_can_make_a_better_ world?language=en on December 15, 2015.

McGonigal, J. (2011a). *Reality is broken: Why games make us better and how they can change the world.* New York: Penguin Press.

McGonigal, J. (2011b, February 15). *Video games: An hour a day is key to success in life.* Accessed at www.huffingtonpost.com/jane-mcgonigal/video-games_b_823208.html on August 25, 2015.

McLeod, S. (2008). Erik Erikson. *SimplyPsychology.* Accessed at www.simplypsychology .org/Erik-Erikson.html on August 1, 2016.

Medina, J. (2009). *Brain rules: 12 principles for surviving and thriving at work, home, and school.* Seattle, WA: Pear Press.

Mid-continent Research for Education and Learning International. (2014). *Content knowledge online edition.* Accessed at www2.mcrel.org/compendium/browse.asp on May 10, 2016.

Miller, R. (2007). Halo 3 garners $170 million in US first day, breaks records. *Engadget.* Accessed at www.engadget.com/2007/09/26/halo-3-nets-170-million-in-us-first-day -breaks-records on May 20, 2015.

MindShift. (2014, November 12). *A third grader's plea for more game-based learning* [Blog post]. Accessed at http://blogs.kqed.org/mindshift/2014/11/a-third-graders-plea-for -more-game-based-learning on January 13, 2015.

Montessori, M. (1936). *The secret of childhood* (B. B. Carter, trans. and ed.). New York: Orient Longman.

Nagel, D. (2014). *One-third of U.S. students use school-issued mobile devices.* Accessed at http://thejournal.com/articles/2014/04/08/a-third-of-secondary-students-use-school -issued-mobile-devices.aspx on May 20, 2015.

National Council for the Social Studies. (2010). *National Curriculum Standards for Social Studies: A framework for teaching, learning, and assessment.* Accessed at www .socialstudies.org/standards on August 5, 2016.

National Education Association. (2012). *Preparing 21st century students for a global society: An educator's guide to the "Four Cs."* Accessed at www.nea.org/assets/docs/A -Guide-to-Four-Cs.pdf on August 18, 2016.

National Governors Association Center for Best Practices & Council of Chief State School Officers. (2010a). *Common Core State Standards Initiative*. Washington, DC: Authors.

National Governors Association Center for Best Practices & Council of Chief State School Officers. (2010b). *Common Core State Standards for English language arts and literacy in history/social studies, science, and technical subjects*. Washington, DC: Authors. Accessed at www.corestandards.org/assets/CCSSI_ELA%20Standards.pdf on January 26, 2016.

National Governors Association Center for Best Practices & Council of Chief State School Officers. (2010c). *Common Core State Standards for mathematics*. Washington, DC: Authors. Accessed at www.corestandards.org/assets/CCSSI_Math%20Standards .pdf on January 26, 2016.

Netop. (2013). *Case story: The move to mobile—Real schools, real stories—Brockport Central School District*. Accessed at www2.netop.com/brockportpdf on May 20, 2015.

Newzoo. (2016, April 21). *The global games market reaches $99.6 billion in 2016, mobile generating 37%*. Accessed at newzoo.com/insights/articles/global-games-market -reaches-99-6-billion-2016-mobile-generating-37 on July 20, 2016.

NGSS Lead States. (2013). *Next Generation Science Standards: For states, by states*. Accessed at www.nextgenscience.org/get-to-know on August 6, 2016.

Nichols, S., & Berliner, D. (2005). *The inevitable corruption of indicators and educators through high-stakes testing*. Tempe: Education Policy Studies Laboratory, Arizona State University. Accessed at http://epsl.asu.edu/epru/documents/EPSL-0503-101-EPRU .pdf on August 5, 2016.

Nielsen. (2012). American families see tablets as playmate, teacher and babysitter. *Newswire*. Accessed at www.nielsen.com/us/en/insights/news/2012/american-families-see-tablets -as-playmate-teacher-and-babysitter.html on May 20, 2015.

Nielsen, J. (2006). *F-shaped pattern for reading web content*. Accessed at www.nngroup .com/articles/f-shaped-pattern-reading-web-content on August 1, 2016.

NPD Group. (2011). *The video game industry is adding 2–17 year-old gamers at a rate higher than that age group's population growth*. Accessed at www.afjv.com/news/233_ kids-and-gaming-2011.htm on February 16, 2015.

NPD Group. (2014). *The NPD Group reports 34 million core gamers spend an average of 22 hours per week playing video games*. Accessed at www.npd.com/wps/portal/npd/us /news/press-releases/the-npd-group-reports-34-million-core-gamers-spend-an-average -of-22-hours-per-week-playing-video-games on May 20, 2015.

Obaid, M. A. S. (2013). The impact of using multi-sensory approach for teaching students with learning disabilities. *Journal of International Education Research, 9*(1), 75–82.

Oskin, B. (2012). Teens and video games: How much is too much? *Live Science*. Accessed at www.livescience.com/22281-teens-video-games-health-risks.html on July 25, 2015.

Papert, S. (2002). *Hard fun*. Accessed at www.papert.org/articles/HardFun.html on May 20, 2015.

Piaget, J. (1962). *Play, dreams, and imitation in childhood*. New York: Norton.

Poh, M.-Z., Swenson, N. C., & Picard, R. W. (2010). A wearable sensor for unobtrusive, long-term assessment of electrodermal activity. *IEEE Transactions on Biomedical Engineering, 57*(5), 1243–1252.

Prensky, M. (2007). *Digital game-based learning* (Re-published ed.). St. Paul, MN: Paragon House.

Provenzo, E. F., Jr. (1991). *Video kids: Making sense of Nintendo*. Cambridge, MA: Harvard University Press.

Rideout, V. (2013). *Zero to eight: Children's media use in America 2013—A Common Sense research study*. San Francisco: Common Sense Media. Accessed at www .commonsensemedia.org/file/zero-to-eight-2013pdf-0/download on January 9, 2015.

Robertson, A. (2014). 'Angry Birds Stella' launches to increase series' 2 billion downloads. *Forbes*. Accessed at www.forbes.com/sites/andyrobertson/2014/09/04/angry-birds -stella-hands-on-review on February 16, 2015.

Robinson, A. (2014, July 22). *150 neurons mapped in EyeWire!* [Blog post]. Accessed at http://blog.eyewire.org/150-neurons-mapped-in-eyewire on September 25, 2015.

Sandford, R., Ulicsak, M., Facer, K., & Rudd, T. (2006). *Teaching with games: Using commercial off-the-shelf computer games in formal education*. Accessed at www.nfer .ac.uk/publications/FUTL49/FUTL49.pdf on February 16, 2015.

Schaaf, R. (2014, March 27). *10 free online educational game sites* [Blog post]. Accessed at http://blogs.kqed.org/mindshift/2014/03/10-free-online-educational-game-sites on January 9, 2017.

Schaaf, R., & Mohan, N. (2014). *Making school a game worth playing: Digital games in the classroom*. Thousand Oaks, CA: Corwin Press.

Schaaf, R. L. (2015). *Using digital games as assessment and instruction tools*. Bloomington, IN: Solution Tree Press.

School Improvement in Maryland. (2016). *State curriculum*. Accessed at http://mdk12 .msde.maryland.gov/instruction/curriculum on August 5, 2016.

Schreier, J. (2010). *'Call of Duty: Black Ops' smashes one-day sales record*. Accessed at www .cnn.com/2010/TECH/gaming.gadgets/11/11/call.of.duty.sales on May 20, 2015.

Shaffer, D. W., Squire, K. R., Halverson, R., & Gee, J. P. (2005). Video games and the future of learning. *Phi Delta Kappan, 87*(2), 104–111.

Shapiro, J., Salen, K., Schwartz, K., & Darvasi, P. (2014). *MindShift guide to digital games + learning.* Accessed at www.kqed.org/assets/pdf/news/MindShift -GuidetoDigitalGamesandLearning.pdf on January 9, 2015.

Shute, V., & Ventura, M. (2013). *Stealth assessment: Measuring and supporting learning in video games.* Cambridge, MA: MacArthur Foundation. Accessed at http://mitpress .mit.edu/books/stealth-assessment on February 16, 2015.

Small, G., & Vorgan, G. (2008). *iBrain: Surviving the technological alteration of the modern mind.* New York: Collins Living.

Statistica. (2014a). *Number of apps available in leading app stores as of July 2014.* New York: Author.

Statistica. (2014b). *Most popular Apple App Store categories in September 2014, by share of available apps.* New York: Author.

Statistica. (2015a). *Global PC and console games revenue in 2014 and 2019 (in billion U.S. dollars).* New York: Author.

Statistica. (2015b). *Number of apps available in leading app stores as of July 2015.* New York: Author.

Stegelin, D. A. (2005). Making the case for play policy: Research-based reasons to support play-based environments. *Young Children, 60*(2), 76–85.

Steiner, C. (2014, October 15). *Individualization, failure, and fun* [Video file]. Accessed at http://tedxtalks.ted.com/video/Individualization-Failure-and-F on January 13, 2015.

Takahashi, D. (2013). *More than 1.2 billion people are playing games.* Accessed at http:// venturebeat.com/2013/11/25/more-than-1-2-billion-people-are-playing-games on August 25, 2015.

Takeuchi, L. M., & Vaala, S. (2014). *Level up learning: A national survey on teaching with digital games.* New York: Joan Ganz Cooney Center at Sesame Workshop. Accessed at www.joanganzcooneycenter.org/wp-content/uploads/2014/10/jgcc_leveluplearning _final.pdf on January 12, 2015.

Taylor, F. W. (1911). *The principles of scientific management.* New York: Harper.

Tercek, R. (2015). *Vaporized: Solid strategies for success in a dematerialized world.* Vancouver, British Columbia, Canada: LifeTree Media.

Thalheimer, W. (2006, February). *Spacing learning events over time: What the research says.* Accessed at www.leerbeleving.nl/wp-content/uploads/2011/11/Spacing_Learning_ Over_Time__March2009v1_.pdf on January 9, 2015.

Toffler, A. (1970). *Future shock.* New York: Random House.

Tutin, D. (2012, November 7). *10 key learning trends for 2013* [Blog post]. Accessed at http://lumesse.typepad.com/lumesse/2012/11/10-key-learning-trends-for-2013.html on July 25, 2015.

University of Colorado Denver. (2010). Video games can be highly effective training tools, study shows: Employees learn more, forget less, master more skills. *ScienceDaily*. Accessed at www.sciencedaily.com/releases/2010/10/101019171854.htm on January 26, 2016.

Video Game Wiki Sales. (2013). *Video game industry*. Accessed at http://vgsales.wikia .com/wiki/Video_game_industry#cite_note-cpi_inflation-92 on May 20, 2015.

Vygotsky, L. S. (1978). *Mind in society: The development of higher psychological processes* (M. Cole, V. John-Steiner, & E. Souberman, eds.) (14th ed.). Cambridge, MA: Harvard University Press.

Wagner, T. (2008). *The global achievement gap: Why even our best schools don't teach the new survival skills our children need—And what we can do about it.* New York: Basic Books.

Walsh, K. (2014). 8 positive findings from 4 year 1:1 iPad initiative. *EmergingEdTech*. Accessed at www.emergingedtech.com/2014/10/8-positive-findings-from-4-year-11-ipad -initiative on August 1, 2016.

Watson, W. R., Watson, S. L., & Reigeluth, C. M. (2012). Education 3.0: Breaking the mold with technology. *Interactive Learning Environments, 23*(3), 332–343.

Whitton, N. (2010). *Learning with digital games: A practical guide to engaging students in higher education.* New York: Routledge.

World Food Programme. (n.d.). Free Rice *2.0 total donations by date.* Accessed at http:// freerice.com/frmisc/totals on October 18, 2016.

Wouters, P., van der Spek, E., & van Oostendorp, H. (n.d.). *Current practices in serious game research: A review from a learning outcome perspective.* Accessed at www.cs.uu.nl /docs/vakken/b3elg/literatuur_files/Wouters.pdf on August 8, 2016.

Zohar, A., & Dori, Y. (2003). Higher order thinking skills and low-achieving students: Are they mutually exclusive? *Journal of the Learning Sciences, 2(12)*,145–188.

INDEX

Reinventing Learning for the Always-On Generation
Ian Jukes, Ryan L. Schaaf, and Nicky Mohan
Cultivate effective 21st century classrooms. Explore the differences in students' neurological processing from previous generations, investigate the nine critical attributes of digital learners, and discover practical strategies for making learning relevant, engaging, and fun through digital activities.
BKF644

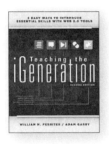

Teaching the iGeneration
William M. Ferriter and Adam Garry
Find the natural overlap between the work you already believe in and the digital tools that define today's learning. Each chapter introduces an enduring life skill and a digital solution to enhance traditional skill-based instructional practices. A collection of handouts and supporting materials ends each chapter.
BKF671

Using Digital Games as Assessment and Instruction Tools
Ryan L. Schaaf
Combine hard work and deep fun in classrooms with digital game–based learning. Discover how to incorporate digital tools and use them to craft engaging, academically applicable classroom activities that address content standards and revitalize learning for both teachers and students.
BKF666

Bring Your Own Device
Kipp D. Rogers
This book shows educators how to incorporate students' personal technology tools into instruction. BYOD allows students to be active participants in their learning and helps teachers equip them with the skills required to be college, career, and citizenship ready.
BKF672

Solution Tree | Press
a division of
Solution Tree

Visit SolutionTree.com or call 800.733.6786 to order.

"Excellent engagement
in what truly matters
in **assessment**.

Great examples!"

—Carol Johnson, superintendent,
Central Dauphin School District, Pennsylvania

 PD Services

Our experts draw from decades of research and their own experiences to bring you
practical strategies for designing and implementing quality assessments. You can choose
from a range of customizable services, from a one-day overview to a multiyear process.

Book your assessment PD today!
888.763.9045

Solution Tree